The Evolution of the
Nursery–Infant School

STUDENTS LIBRARY OF EDUCATION

The Evolution of the Nursery–Infant School

A History of Infant and Nursery Education in Britain, 1800-1970

Nanette Whitbread
Leicester College of Education

LONDON AND BOSTON

ROUTLEDGE & KEGAN PAUL

First published 1972
by Routledge & Kegan Paul Ltd,
Broadway House, 68-74 Carter Lane,
London EC4V 5EL and
9 Park Street,
Boston, Mass. 02108, U.S.A.

Printed in Great Britain by
Northumberland Press Ltd,
Gateshead

ISBN 0 7100 7290 2 (c)
       0 7100 7291 0 (p)

THE STUDENTS LIBRARY OF EDUCATION has been designed to meet the needs of students of Education at Colleges of Education and at University Institutes and Departments. It will also be valuable for practising teachers and educationists. The series takes full account of the latest developments in teacher-training and of new methods and approaches in education. Separate volumes will provide authoritative and up-to-date accounts of the topics within the major fields of sociology, philosophy and history of education, educational psychology, and method. Care has been taken that specialist topics are treated lucidly and usefully for the non-specialist reader. Altogether, the Students Library of Education will provide a comprehensive introduction and guide to anyone concerned with the study of education, and with educational theory and practice.

J. W. TIBBLE

A history of infant education by R. R. Rusk was published in 1933. Little or nothing has been written on the subject since, except in the relation to the theory and practice of such outstanding figures as Pestalozzi, Froebel, Montessori —or of that pioneer of the infant school, Robert Owen of New Lanark. The merit of this book is that it considers the actual development of infant schools and education in Britain against the background of industrialization and social change, making clear how this development was influenced by the ideas of particular theorists from both the continent and England.

The British infant school is a unique institution, in so far as most continental countries begin formal schooling at six or seven rather than five. But there were also many more children under five in the elementary schools of the nineteenth century than is usually realized. As the rigidity of the elementary school was broken down, so there were more opportunities to develop appropriate methods for teaching the youngest children. But, at the same time, the tendency in the early twentieth century was to exclude from the schools those under five. Then the nursery school was born, and a new history began of devising an appropriate environment and activities for the children from the age of three.

In this book, Nanette Whitbread has made a contribution to the history of primary education which will interest all students of education and suggest a number of fruitful issues which deserve to be followed up.

BRIAN SIMON

Contents

Tables

Preface

In the last few decades there has been growing recognition of the importance of the pre-school and infant years in a child's intellectual development. For this and a number of other, largely social, reasons the demand for nursery education has increased among all social classes. These considerations make this an appropriate time to examine the historical evolution of nursery and infant education in Britain. Previous histories of infant education have focused on the ideas of the great educators without paying much attention to the development of the infant school, and there has been little historical consideration of pre-school provision. This study attempts to reappraise the influence of individual theorists on the kind of education given to young children, to analyse sociological factors that determined need and demand for nursery provision, and to assess the effects of voluntary enterprise and official policies.

Content and method in nursery and infant schools have been subject to conflicting traditions. The idea of fostering the child's natural development was derived from Rousseau and, particularly as interpreted by Froebelians, struggled for acceptance against pressures for early formal instruction in, or in preparation for, elementary and private schools. Social rescue and physical welfare alone tended to motivate nursery care, but the idea of nursery education consistent with the developmental tradition slowly gained acceptance. Nursery-infant education came to be seen as a continuum. Child-centred developmentalists for some time resisted structured learning based on research concerning cognitive and linguistic development, but gradually accepted it for the infant stage while for long continuing to question its validity for nursery education.

Until quite recently it was generally assumed that children under about five or six years old should be at home with their mothers; but in practice, ever since the start of the Industrial Revolution, very young children of working mothers were left with child-minders or sent to school with older brothers and sisters. The practical origin of nursery-infant education in the last century was in babies' classes of elementary schools, separate schools for twos to sevens supposedly modelled on Robert Owen's at New Lanark, and middle-class Froebelian kindergartens. From early in this century the need for nurseries in slum districts was recognized, but provision has been negligible except in war-time. More under-fives were accommodated in infant schools, even when official policy kept numbers to a minimum, than in separate nursery schools. Infant teachers, particularly in certain parts of the country, have been empirically evolving nursery-infant education for over a century.

A review of national trends inevitably hides local variations, though the most significant of these have been noted in this study. Statistics have been given when available to demonstrate trends in provision for children under five:

those in special and hospital schools have not been included, and until 1969 no information was available about many small private nurseries.

Today the demand for nursery education greatly exceeds provision in both maintained and private sectors, and there is danger that the relatively faster growth of the latter may promote greater social inequalities in educational achievement than result anyway from differences of home background. The English infant school evolved as a unique institution, widely acclaimed, but its success continues to be undermined by restrictive policies towards nursery education.

Among the many people who have helped me in this study I should particularly like to thank Miss M. H. Saul, Librarian of the Froebel Educational Institute, who kindly made published and unpublished documents available to me, and my ex-colleague Mrs K. Douet for her invaluable advice, criticism and encouragement.

N.E.M.W.

Part One

The Nineteenth Century

1

Industrialization and philanthropy: 1800-40

In pre-industrial England, as in any rural society, children were gradually introduced to work as they grew up. Their parents and older brothers or sisters taught them useful skills at an early age, and in upper-class families the mother traditionally taught her children to read by the time they were four or five. Quite young children helped with farm work, household chores and domestic crafts in families of all social classes below the aristocracy. Folk-lore, Bible stories, proverbs, ballads, rustic rites and dances were learnt at home and through the seasonal pattern of village life. When their help was not required in the business of earning a living, children of all ages went to the local free grammar or village school that existed in many market towns and the larger villages, and attendance under eight was not uncommon. Since these were single classroom schools there was no special provision for the youngest.

Child labour

The economic and social changes of the agricultural and industrial revolutions from the middle years of the eighteenth century profoundly affected family life, particularly for the poorest families. Pauper children from the workhouses were the first victims as they were no longer the responsibility of their parents but of the Poor Law guardians. Child labour was introduced in the cotton mills by supplying employers with pauper 'apprentices', from London and other urban parishes, under contract from the age of five, six or seven. By the terms of the first Factory Act passed in 1802, these children were not supposed to work more than twelve hours a day and were to be given some instruction in reading, writing and arithmetic on week-days, with religious instruction on Sundays. This Act aroused a storm of protest from employers and was not generally enforced: child apprentices continued to work a seventy-four hour week. By the early nineteenth century migration to the factory towns was making available local supplies of 'free' factory children who were the responsibility of their own parents, and who were not covered by even the ineffective 1802 Act.

This was a much harsher form of child labour than that which had prevailed under the domestic system of cottage industry, even when parents had been hard task-masters. These children worked a six-day week from five or six in the morning till seven or eight at night, or longer at busy times of year, and brutal discipline was used to keep them from flagging. Their wages were essential to the family income. In the village they had worked under the surveillance of their parents, but in factories and mines this was not so.

As the new conditions of child labour began to be made known there was a gradual awakening of the public conscience. Two Parliamentary enquiries were undertaken

4

and their Reports published : *The Report of the Committee appointed to examine the Number and State of Parish Apprentices* (1814-15) and *The Report on Children Employed in Manufactories* (1816). These revealed that, though some age between eight and ten was the more usual for children to begin work, there were many instances of much younger children as factory workers. Other contemporary accounts showed that young child labour was not confined to factories. 'Climbing boys' were taken by chimney sweeps as young as three or four, because only such small children could climb inside the narrow, angled chimneys. Others were employed at home on piece-work put out by the local factory.

As child labour began to be seen as an inhuman outrage, efforts were directed towards restricting it and providing elementary day schools. At least with regard to young children there is some justice in the claim that 'The rescue-motive lay at the root of popular instruction' (Dobbs, 1919, 113). Equally important was the sense of religious or moral mission combined with the social purpose of training in disciplined obedience. As the Factory Commissioners recognized some years later, merely to prohibit child labour 'might be productive of more evil from disorderly habits incident to idleness than of good by rescue from excessive labour' unless a positive alternative was provided (*P.P.*, 1834, xix, 273).

The two original organizations to found day schools for working-class children were the British and Foreign Schools Society and the National Society for Promoting the Education of the Poor in the Principles of the Established Church throughout England and Wales. The former was formed in 1814 through the reorganization of the undenominational Society founded in 1808 by Joseph Lancaster's friends, and the National Society was formed by Dr Bell and his Church of England associates in 1811. Government action was confined to investigations into child labour and an enquiry 'into the Education of the Lower Orders' in London in 1816 and the rest of Britain in 1818. Whenever popular education was discussed in Parliament, 'school age' was defined as six to twelve or seven to thirteen, usually the latter; and this was the age range for whom the voluntary societies aimed to provide schools.

Monitorial schools

The need to run schools as cheaply as possible caused the societies to adopt the mutual or monitorial system for instruction. In one large schoolroom hundreds of children of various ages and standards of attainment were taught with only one master in charge, as child monitors taught ten to twenty children each. These monitors were the older children of nine or above, and only they were taught by the master. Children sat in serried rows on wooden benches, learning by heart what their monitors taught them. This was the factory system of mass production applied to instruction.

The method was intended for children over seven, but some monitorial schools later included children from as young as four (P.P., 1834, ix, 7). Lancaster had seen the need for 'initiatory' schools for children under seven who could there be trained in good social and moral habits in preparation for the monitorial school, and be kept in safety off the streets. But such schools were not founded by either society. The Secretary of the British and Foreign Schools Society said that children came to school 'at all ages between six and twelve' (P.P., 1834, ix, 24), but the National Society for long resisted admission under seven. The societies aimed to provide instruction not nurseries.

Dame schools

Supporters of the voluntary societies had little knowledge

6

of the circumstances in which children under seven were being brought up in working-class districts. Growing up in the overcrowded and insanitary conditions of slum dwellings, their working mothers away from home for perhaps two-thirds of each twenty-four hours, these children were inevitably victims of neglect. Most working-class children of that time can have experienced little of a mother's care during their formative early years. Moreover, there was a marked increase in the number of children under five years of age as the high rate of infant mortality fell around 1800.

A working mother with young children had to make such arrangements as she could. She could leave them in the slum tenement, alone or in the care of a slightly older child. She might find a neighbour, 'some little girl or aged woman, who is hired for a trifle and whose services are equivalent to the reward' (P.P., 1933, xx). Not to work herself was seldom a viable economic alternative, though she might in some districts be able to do piece-work at home. The most common solution was a dame school.

A neighbour, as a paid child-minder, would take as many small children as could be crowded into her tenement or cellar. These premises were likely to be unhealthy, dirty and ill-ventilated. The woman in charge might be a homely, kindly person who was too crippled or otherwise ailing for factory work; if she had had any formal education herself she tried to give some instruction in the alphabet and reading during part of the long day when the children were in her care. Others were unscrupulous and uncaring, concerned only to collect the fees of 2d to 7d a week. Such were the varied circumstances of the urban dame schools, of which there were over 3,000 by 1819 (P.P., 1820, xii, 343).

The dame school can be classified as mutual self-help arising within working-class culture in the early industrial era. In this respect it may be compared with the widespread development of unregistered childminding of pre-school children in the mid-twentieth century. The *laissez-faire* philosophy of the nineteenth century did not allow for government intervention in such domestic matters.

An infant school movement

From the 1820s an infant school movement began to provide an alternative to these *ad hoc* arrangements for children between about two and seven years of age. As already noted, Joseph Lancaster had envisaged 'initiatory' schools. Throughout the nineteenth century the Nonconformist conscience was more readily awakened to the plight of infants in the slums than was the Anglican, perhaps because at this age children were susceptible to moral training but not to doctrinal teaching. The Evangelical wing of the Church of England proved willing to co-operate with Nonconformists in the founding of infant schools 'because of their belief in child conversion' (Burgess, 1958).

In England the promoters' motives were moral and social rescue, reduction of petty crime against property, and early training and discipline. Lord Brougham declared that he considered 'the establishment of infant schools one of the most important improvements—I was going to say in education, but I ought rather to say in the civil polity of this country'. In Scotland, where the influence of Robert Owen and David Stow worked within an older and more democratic tradition of popular education, there was more concern for broad educational aims appropriate to very young children.

New Lanark Infant School

The first infant school in Britain was opened in 1816 at the New Lanark cotton mills by the Welsh manager,

Robert Owen. Under the previous management 'between 400 and 500 pauper children, procured from parishes, whose ages appeared to be from five to ten' (Owen, 1857, *see* Silver, 1969) had been employed as 'apprentices'; but Owen ended this system, so that by the time he opened his infant school the children were those of New Lanark mill workers.

Education and social reform were inextricably linked for Robert Owen. His educational theory was influenced by John Locke (1632-1704), and he had visited the schools of the Swiss pioneers Pestalozzi (1746-1827) and von Fellenberg (1771-1844). Unlike the Radicals, who supported him without accepting his philosophy, he wanted to use education as an instrument for social change whereby a new form of socialist society would replace the existing competitive, class-structured one (Owen, 1813):

> This experiment at New Lanark was the first commencement of practical measures with a view to change the fundamental principle on which society has theretofore been based from the beginning; and no experiment could be more successful in proving the truth of the principle that the character is formed *for* and not *by* the individual (Owen, 1857).

Essentially an environmentalist, his fundamental educational theory was summarized in *The New Moral World* (1836) under 'Five Fundamental Facts', of which the following two were crucial:

> 1. Man is a compound being, whose character is formed of his constitution or organization at birth, and of the effects of external circumstances acting upon that organization, which effects continue to operate upon and to influence him from birth to death.
> 5. Nevertheless, the constitution of every infant, except in the case of organic disease, is capable of being formed or matured, either into a *very inferior*, or a *very superior* being, according to the qualities of the

external circumstances allowed to influence that constitution from birth.

He tried to provide social training in an educationally stimulating environment suited to the age and interests of the children in his infant school at New Lanark. By contemporary standards his school was child-centred, and it can be justly described as the first in the developmental tradition of primary education. This account is taken from his autobiography by A. L. Morton (1962, p. 103), where Owen explained the instructions he gave to the two untrained teachers, James Buchanan and Molly Young:

> they were on no account ever to beat any one of the children, or to threaten them in any manner of word or action, or to use abusive terms; but were always to speak to them with a pleasant countenance, and in a kind manner and tone of voice. That they should tell the infants and children (for they had all from one to six years old under their charge) that they must on all occasions do all they could to make their play-fellows happy ... The schoolroom ... was furnished with paintings, chiefly of animals, with maps, and often supplied with natural objects from the gardens, fields and woods—the examination and explanation of which always excited their curiosity and created an animated conversation between the children and their instructors ...

Singing, dancing, marching to music, fife-playing and geography featured in this infant school curriculum from which books were excluded, and the children spent three hours in the open playground. In effect, it was a combined nursery–infant school, but later the four- to six-year-olds were given a separate room from the two- to four-year-olds. At six or seven children moved to the schoolroom. They left school for the mill when they were ten. The school was part of Owen's model factory settlement with workers' flats, canteen, recreational facilities and an evening institute.

Infant school societies

The New Lanark Infant School attracted many visitors. Among them was the Radical Member of Parliament, Henry Brougham. As a result, he and other Radicals sponsored the first English infant school, opened in 1818 at Brewer's Green in Westminster, with James Buchanan as master. In 1820 Samuel Wilderspin was appointed master of the second opened at Spitalfields by Brougham's friend Joseph Wilson; his brother, the vicar of Walthamstow, was responsible for the third in 1824. Unlike Owen's at New Lanark, these London infant schools were in the poorest urban environment: this may partly account for the transformation of the English model into a much more rigid instrument for instruction and discipline, where Owen's methods were divorced from his concept of education and community welfare. Moreover, the Walthamstow school was intended to prepare children for the National Society school at seven.

By 1824 enough interest had been aroused in infant schools for the London Infant School Society to be formed, with the object of training infant teachers. A site was never found for the proposed modern school where students were to practise teaching, and the lack of any infant teacher training in England remained a major problem. The Society did much to promote the founding of further infant schools and continued to advertise till 1828, but had ceased its activities by 1835.

Local infant school societies were formed in several industrial towns, as in Leicester in 1828. There the project nearly foundered on the denominational issue, one High Tory clergyman 'objecting to children being taken from their parents' care at so early an age' (Patterson, 1954, 161).

Dissenters were usually more prominent than members of the Established Church in promoting infant schools, but the religious issue was seldom a serious obstacle and many local societies were inter-denominational. The London adaptations of the infant school were the models which local societies copied, for they were described in manuals written in the 1820s for the guidance of infant teachers by Samuel Wilderspin of Spitalfields, Rev. William Wilson of Walthamstow, and were the main source of Dr Thomas Pole's authoritative *Observations Relative to Infant Schools* (1823). David Goyder, who also wrote manuals, ran an infant school at Meadow Street, Bristol, that seems to have been more like Owen's New Lanark model.

In Glasgow, David Stow, who was already concerned with moral rescue and social training of young slum children in his Sunday School, realized that an infant day school would provide a more effective means of achieving his object and applying his educational ideas. He formed the Glasgow Infant School Society about 1826-8, opened the Drygate Infant School in April 1828 and began training infant teachers. He advocated simultaneous or class instruction but stressed understanding rather than mere memorizing, and made great use of the playground with a giant stride and wooden building bricks. He anticipated Froebel (see chapter 3) in his appreciation of spontaneous play, and understood Owen's aims better than the various English exponents of infant teaching.

Samuel Wilderspin (1792-1866)

The great promoter of infant schools in England was Samuel Wilderspin. He had been master of Spitalfields Infant School before becoming the tireless agent of the London Infant School Society. He knew Robert Owen, James Buchanan and David Stow, but he and Owen became bitterly hostile later on and each maligned the other in jealous disputes over who originated the infant school.

Wilderspin toured the country giving lectures and staying a couple of weeks in a town to help start a local infant school. Largely through his efforts 150 infant schools were opened in about ten years: in Manchester there were five with a total of 743 on roll, and three in Salford. He wrote several manuals on infant teaching, but the methods he advocated bore little resemblance to those practised at New Lanark. However, his lectures and manuals were very influential so that his, not Owen's, was the model for infant schools during the next twenty years. *On the Importance of Educating the Infant Children of the Poor*, first published in 1823, was reprinted eight times under varying titles. In this he explained the purpose of the tiered infant 'gallery' which he invented so that little children could sit where they could see and be seen by the teacher as he instructed them by practical demonstration, questioning and frequent use of a variety of visual aids. Much of the teaching he recommended was practical, particularly in arithmetic for which he devised ingenious apparatus, but it also included instructional rhymes and rules and a good deal of verbal repetition. Infants 'should spend at least half the school time' in a playground equipped with a revolving swing, ropes for jumping over and wooden building blocks, and complete with flower-beds and trees.

Unlike Owen, he was concerned to adapt elementary instruction to the capacities of very young children. Consequently his system relied on 'books, lessons and apparatus' and rote learning. He divorced the infant school movement from the new developmental approach introduced by Owen, and instead brought it within the instructional tradition of the elementary school. This was epitomized by his coaching 'infant prodigies' who demonstrated the success of infant schools on his lecture tours.

The lack of any unifying pedagogical theory was Wilderspin's great weakness. His practical experience had given him remarkable insight into young children's thinking and behaviour, and he appreciated the teacher's role in fostering their natural curiosity and developing sensory perception; but he was inconsistent, too empirical and eclectic, without the intellectual ability to analyse and synthesize the various ideas and methods which he made use of and recommended to others.

Conflicting aims

Part of Samuel Wilderspin's inconsistency may be attributed to his failure to understand the conflicting social and political philosophies of his contemporaries. Robert Owen was a Utopian socialist whose educational theory was integral to his hope of a classless society and 'a new character for the human race' (Owen, 1836, ch. 9); hence he insisted that from their earliest years children should learn to co-operate with one another and become reasonable human beings. Even in the short term at New Lanark he hoped to effect a regeneration among the working population. But Wilderspin rejected this link between education and social change. Nor did he accept the reformist conservatism of traditional philanthropists.

Religious teaching had no place in Owen's school but featured prominently in Wilderspin's manuals and all subsequent infant schools. From 1824 the New Lanark Schools were taken over by the British and Foreign Schools Society, and a year later the London Infant School Society came under Anglican control. However, the early infant schools largely escaped inter-denominational controversy.

It is understandable that infant teachers felt the pressure to begin formal instruction as young as possible when schooling was often cut short by juvenile employment at eight or nine. Particularly among the unskilled and casually employed, parents could not afford to do without their children's earnings; and employers continued to take advantage of cheap child labour so long as children's skills could be used in the early phase of mechanized industry. Infant teachers in England had had no training courses on the needs of early childhood, and the more conscientious felt that the best they could do was to prepare their infant classes for the discipline of the monitorial school.

Many infant schools became merely initiatory to the monitorial school as the techniques of the latter were adapted to mass instruction of children aged two to seven. This was Wilderspin's contribution to the problem of teaching large numbers while following Owen in rejecting the monitorial method of mutual instruction; simultaneous instruction was a feature of all infant schools, but this meant firm discipline and rote learning. This was also the policy of the Rev. William Wilson of Walthamstow who 'injected into the infant school situation the function of *preparation*, preparation for entry into National Schools' (Silver, 1965, 143). Henry Dunn, Secretary of the British and Foreign Schools Society, clearly regarded this as the proper purpose of good infant schools when he deplored that too often 'infant schools tuition is so much amusement that the children are not willing at first to work, or to make a serious business of their studies' on entry to the British school (*P.P.*, 1834, ix, 30). Under such pressure the half day in the playground was apt to be abandoned.

Dunn's complaint, however, showed that many working-class parents were very willing to send their children to those infant schools that put little emphasis on instruction and discipline. For he went on to say : 'It is very easy to open an infant school, and to introduce certain amusements for the children' (*P.P.*, 1834, ix, 30). Naturally, parents would chose an infant school that offered some amusements for the children rather than mere minding in an urban dame school, which was usually the only alternative.

Robert Owen's socialist educational theory persisted

within the labour movement and his concept of an infant school was revived by the Chartists in the 1840s (Lovett & Collins, 1841). In the 1830s attempts were made to include his kind of infant school as part of some Mechanics' Institutes, but success was very limited (Silver, 1965). Infant schools of the 1820s, like most popular education, was provided *for*, not *by*, the working-classes.

Though the Owenite concept of infant education was eroded, the idea of a separate infant school for children under seven became accepted as philanthropists realized that these young children were at risk in the industrial slums. And despite their weaknesses the new infant schools were more humane that monitorial schools or many dame schools.

2

Advance and setback: 1836-62

Although many infant schools had been started in the 1820s there was no clear concept of infant education: its definition depended solely on the age of the children. Strict discipline, formal instruction and much rote learning characterized both monitorial and infant schools, though there was more use of visual aids and recitation of rhyming rules in the latter. Infant school practice differed from monitorial only in substituting simultaneous or mass instruction of the whole class by the teacher: but the reason was a practical not a theoretical one—the oldest infants, being only seven years, were too young to use as monitors.

New educational theory from the Continent was slow in reaching England. Rousseau's *Emile* (1762) had interested some of the liberal-minded middle class, but his revolutionary political ideas and his rejection of original sin made his writings unacceptable to conservative Anglicans.

Among those who were strongly influenced by Rousseau's educational ideas was the Edgeworth family in Ireland. Richard Lovell Edgeworth brought his first child up on the principles of *Emile* until he was eight, and his second wife started a register of detailed observations on their children, which her husband continued through his later marriages. The outcome of this was *Practical Education*, written jointly with his novelist daughter, Maria, and published in 1798. Intended as advice to ambitious parents of the rising middle class on how to bring up their children before sending them to a public or grammar school at eight or nine, it emphasized active learning by experiment with real things, explained the educational value of certain nursery toys and enunciated 'the general principle that we should associate pleasure with whatever we wish that our pupils should pursue, and pain with whatever we wish that they should avoid' (Edgeworth, 1822 ed., 158). A new appreciation of children's play was implicit throughout and was made explicit in a long paragraph on the subject: 'If by play be meant everything that is not usually called a task, then undoubtedly much may be learned at play ... but from the moment the attention is fixed, no matter on what, children are no longer at idle play, they are at active work' (1822 ed., 81-2).

This book contained the beginnings of an infant pedagogy for promoting the individual child's mental development in an educative home environment. It evoked an immediate response among important sections of the middle class, and had run to a fourth edition by 1822. Middle-class interest in educational theory and practice, apparent in the increasing number of articles in journals, led many to look abroad for new ideas as visits to Europe and publication of information from there became possible after Waterloo. Among the foreign educators who aroused particular interest was Pestalozzi in Switzerland.

Pestalozzi (1745-1827)

Like R. L. Edgeworth, Johann Heinrich Pestalozzi had been disillusioned when he tried to bring his own son up on Emilian principles, but he remained much influenced by Rousseau's theories, which he carried further. Pestalozzi took from Rousseau the conviction that education must harmonize with the child's nature. His approach was child-centred in that he aimed to take account of the child's interests and capabilities, but he in no way abdicated from the teacher's responsibility to direct children's learning. Although he never wrote a comprehensive description of his theories and methods, he tried empirically to devise a system of teaching that was determined by the child's capacity at each stage of development. In his *Report of the Method* (1800), written from his brief experience as an elementary school teacher in Burgdorf, he said: 'I am trying to psychologise the instruction of mankind.' This was what he continued to do at the new school in Yverdun castle from 1805.

He broke his teaching material down into simple steps and based all his elementary education on the three elements of language, number and form. Particularly important was his emphasis on observation leading to verbalization so that children would more readily form concepts. This was the essence of the typically Pestalozzian 'Object Lesson' which became so stereotyped and meaningless in the hands of teachers who did not understand the underlying theory. When he urged 'teach by THINGS', he wanted the children first to discover all they could through their own senses before being told of the object's qualities, origin and use. In number work objects should be used to represent units and children should be questioned and set to solve problems in their own way rather than be told how to find the right answer. He strongly condemned rote learning and fact cramming.

Pestalozzi was not exclusively, or even mainly, concerned with teaching infants; but his greatest contribution in Britain was in the field of infant education. He was a humanitarian rather than a social reformer, and saw education for self-fulfilment as the means by which industrial workers might regain their humanity. Most of his teaching experience was at the castle school in Yverdun, but he believed that his principles had universal application for teaching children from all social classes.

It was at Yverdun that the many foreign visitors saw his new teaching methods. The school was already world-famous before the ending of the Napoleonic Wars made it possible for people from the British Isles to go there. From then until his death Pestalozzi received a stream of British visitors, among whom a significant number was sufficiently impressed to found schools based on Pestalozzian principles on their return and later to write about his methods.

Those more concerned with the political than the pedagogical aspect of education, such as Dr Bell and Lord Brougham, preferred von Fellenberg's school at Hofwyl where the social classes were rigidly segregated and given a largely vocational education. Initially, Pestalozzi's admirers opened preparatory schools for the middle-classes —Dr Charles Edward Orpen's at Birkenhead, James Pierrepoint Greaves' at Ham, Elizabeth and Charles Mayo's at Epsom. The only Pestalozzian elementary school was opened by John H. Synge in County Wicklow, Ireland. They all tried in vain to persuade Pestalozzi to write about his theory and practice or edit his scattered essays so that they might publish an English edition. Eventually, J. P. Greaves, who had been secretary to the London Infant School Society, published a collection of thirty-four letters that Pestalozzi had written to him between 1818 and 1819, *Letters on Early Education* (1827), which ran into several editions. The others all published material about him and his method.

These were the only immediately feasible ways of making Pestalozzi's ideas known in England. Greaves had tried unsuccessfully to interest the Prime Minister, Lord Liverpool, in a scheme for sending English boys to Yverdun to train as teachers. As early as 1818 a group of enthusiasts had tried to raise a public subscription to finance a 'plan for preparing schoolmasters and schoolmistresses for the people' under Pestalozzi's direction, and in the same year Dr Charles Mayo took a party of English students to Yverdun. A few of the original masters of the infant schools of the 1820s had read about Pestalozzi's methods, notably James Buchanan and David Goyder, but none of them had the advantage of seeing Pestalozzi's own school nor of being trained by those who had.

The Home and Colonial Infant School Society

The new private schools attracted a good deal of attention. The Mayos had to move theirs to a larger house at Cheam. In accordance with Pestalozzi's own aim, some of his followers were anxious to liberalize popular education. There was little hope of changing the monitorial schools, committed as these were to the mutual system of instruction; but several key figures in the Pestalozzian movement had been associated with the earlier infant school movement and were particularly interested in promoting infant schools. The Secretary of the British and Foreign Schools Society had complained to the Select Committee, which was then investigating popular education, that there was no institution for training infant teachers (P.P., 1834, ix, 30). Hence, the Home and Colonial Infant School Society was formed in 1836 and on June 1st opened a training college in Holborn.

The leading figures in the formation of the new Society

were J. P. Greaves, J. S. Reynolds, Charles and Elizabeth Mayo. The latter wrote students' manuals on Pestalozzian methodology and her brother lectured on the courses. Initially these training courses were concentrated into six months, but were later extended. By 1843 the college, which had moved to Gray's Inn Road after two years, was training 100 infant teachers a year. The Society then invited inspection by the Committee of Council on Education, and in 1846 received a government grant.

The effect of the Society's work both in training infant teachers and in publicizing Pestalozzi's methods was apparent by the 1840s. Inspectors made a distinction between 'the more modern infant schools' and the rest where the teachers' lack of training was deplored. The opening of a new infant school in Derby under teachers trained by the Society was noted as 'a most favourable omen' (Minutes, 1846, 179). Such was the Society's progress in ten years that Joseph Fletcher reported to the Committee of Council: 'the Home and Colonial Infant School Society is required to supply trained teachers for nearly the whole of the current appointments' (Minutes, 1846, 226). On the other hand, the monitorial system was being imported into infant schools which retained a few children up to nine to 'serve as monitors of little reading classes, and ... even as occasional baby-teachers' (Minutes, 1846, 222).

The age of steam-power

By mid-century there were not only many more infant schools but also a great increase in the number of children under seven attending elementary schools. This requires some explanation, for it was not the result of any campaign.

The period from the middle 1830s can be described as the second phase of the Industrial Revolution. This was the steam age—steam-power for factories and the new

22

railways. There was consequently a massive and accelerated redistribution of population to the new factory towns which had been growing up near the coalfields since 1813 in Lancashire and 1826 in Yorkshire, while the railways opened up the interior of the country and promoted the growth of light industry. By 1840 the urban population was double the rural, and in the five years after 1846 over 3,600 miles of railway line were opened. Irish immigration added a further three per cent to the population by 1851 and the total population of Britain rose from 16,261,000 in 1831 to 20,816,000 in 1851. This phenomenal increase over twenty years clearly included a substantial rise in both numbers and proportion of children as the birth-rate rose and there was no significant fall in the death-rate: a quarter of the population was under ten years old. Working-class living conditions worsened in the overcrowded and insanitary jerry-built slums around each new factory. Over three million were added to the numbers living in towns of 20,000 or more in these two decades. In the first phase of rapid industrial expansion skilled workers' real wages actually fell, but rose fairly steadily for thirty years from about 1842 (Cole & Postgate, 1938). This was the class most able to seek improved facilities for the care of their young children.

If even slightly more money was available in the family it would not be surprising that working mothers were 'ready to make a sacrifice of some pence per week' (Minutes, 1846, 216) to send any children over two or three years old to the safety and cleanliness of an infant school. Infant school fees ranged from a penny to twopence a week, which was about half what most dame schools charged. Worsening slum conditions inevitably brought materially worse dame schools: some of the most deplorable conditions were described by the Inspector for Lancashire (Minutes, 1840, 160-2). In course of time the better infant schools drove out the dame schools, but as

23

yet there were simply not enough of them.

Pressure was increased on the monitorial schools to admit children under seven. No doubt this was partly the result of the progress that had been made in restricting child labour. The first effective Factory Act (1833) prohibited employment of children under nine in textile mills: in 1842 this was extended to children under ten in the coal-mines, in the 1860s to various other industries including pottery works and match factories, and in 1867 to all factories employing more than fifty workers. In any case, increased mechanization of industry meant that there were fewer tasks for which child labour could be used. But if a working mother wanted to send her seven- to ten-year-old to school she was left with the problem of what to do with her younger children: much the easiest solution was to send them along too. As Matthew Arnold found when he was inspecting elementary schools in the 1850s, 'parents will not send the older children without sending these also' (Marvin, 1908, 14). By 1861 it was estimated that 19·8 per cent of children between the ages of three and six were attending public elementary schools (Skeats, 1861, 147).

Babies' classes

Inspectors reported that the presence of large numbers of under-sevens in the elementary school hindered efficient teaching of the older children, and they consequently recommended that provision should be made in another room for a separate 'babies' class'. Most inspectors and teachers did not want to exclude these younger children, not only because to do so would have had the effect of driving older brothers and sisters away to mind them at home, but also because attendance was so irregular even above seven that it seemed desirable to take every advantage of the chance to start elementary education earlier. The

Parliamentary Committee on Education in 1838 expressed the view that educational provision was desirable from the age of three for working-class children. The improved infant schools had convinced many inspectors of the value of a separate infant stage, even 'if they did nothing but contribute to their health and cheerfulness' (Minutes, 1940, 166). For these reasons the Committee of Council 'directed that a collateral series of plans of school-houses should be drawn, in which an infant school and playground are added to the schoolroom for children above six years of age, in the hope that these plans may promote the adoption of arrangements ... for the combination of an infant school with the boys' and girls' school' (Minutes, 1840, 48).

There was ambiguity as to the purpose of infant education. Social and moral rescue from the evils of a slum environment was important and carried the corollary of emphasis on training in good habits of discipline, cleanliness and duty to God. The notion of learning through play had won enough general acceptance to be mentioned in the 1841 *Penny Encyclopaedia*, and the *Glasgow Herald* of 1835 reported: 'They seldom sit on their seats more than fifteen minutes at a time without exercise. All is joyous activity—only pictures and objects are in use, and one-third of their time is spent in amusements in the playground.' Inspectors in England hoped for rather more instruction: 'To read an easy little narrative lesson, have the first notions of numbers, and be able to write on a slate' (Minutes, 1846, 235). Infant schools in England and Scotland by mid-century had certain characteristic features. The schoolroom was a large hall complete with gallery for simultaneous instruction, and the walls were lined with black boarding for the children to draw and write on. A playground, equipped with such apparatus as swings and see-saws, was required in any new infant school applying for grant. The curriculum included drawing, music, physical exercises, sewing, knitting, gardening, at least the preliminary steps towards reading and some-times writing, and Pestalozzian 'object lessons' on natural objects and domestic utensils. *Circular no. 1*, issued by the Committee of Council in 1839, required these physical and curricular provisions for new infant schools if a grant was to be made. The training of more infant teachers was encouraged when the Committee began to offer a supplementary grant to training schools that provided 'a separate and complete course of training for females in-tended to take charge of infant schools' (Minutes, 1854, 33).

The Royal Commission investigating elementary educa-tion in 1861 found that 'if two children enter an elemen-tary school at the age of seven, one coming from a good infant school, the other uneducated, the child from the infant school will make as much progress by the age of ten as the other will by the age of twelve' (Skeats, 1861, 59).

Progress in the expansion and development of infant education seemed assured when a serious setback occurred with the 1862 Revised Code, which introduced the admini-strative principle of payment by results.

The Revised Code

Although the Newcastle Commission (1861) had declared that infant schools were an important part of a national education system, the Code of 1862 fixed the maximum grant-earning capacity of children under six at six shillings and sixpence each as against the twelve shillings for older children, and required inspectors to ensure that the teach-ing of infants did not interfere with the instruction of the others. Infants under six were 'not required to be in-dividually examined', a general report on the class being sufficient; but those over six had to submit to individual, oral examination in reading. R. R. Rusk has contended that 'the Revised Code, by fixing the age of six, disrupted the Infant School and sounded the death-knell of infant education' (1933, 183); but as the original Standard I at six was abandoned ten years later when the old Standard II became Standard I at seven, it seems more likely that the damage was caused rather by backwash on the whole infant stage from examination pressures. Inevitably there was pressure on teachers, whose salaries depended on the amount of grant earned by their pupils, to begin preparing five- and six-year-olds for the Standard examination in the three Rs.

Contrary to the enlightened theory of infant education that had been steadily gaining ground through the Home and Colonial Infant School Society's promotion of Pestalozzian methods, rote learning became firmly entrenched in infant schools for many decades. In these circumstances the new theories of Froebel could not penetrate infant education in elementary schools. The instructional tradition remained dominant, resistant to influence from child-centred developmentalists. But infant schools were at least providing the benefit of a protective environment, mainly for children of the more prosperous skilled working class whose parents could pay the fee.

3

The middle-class kindergarten: 1850-1900

The new middle class

By the middle of the nineteenth century the expanding middle classes, and particularly the professional and business upper middle class, was beginning to seek new ways of educating their own children of infant age. The Industrial Revolution had brought consequent commercial expansion and with this a growth of the professional middle class, whose percentage in the total population of Britain rose from under 2·5 per cent in 1851 to 4·5 per cent twenty years later. When the Taunton Commissioners enquired into secondary education in 1864-8 they recognized that their needs were almost identical to those of the upper class whose sons attended the nine public schools. Since families of this emergent class owed their rise in status to a combination of capital and education, a sound preschool preparation between the ages of about four and eight or nine was recognized as highly advantageous. In upper-class families the mother had traditionally taught her children to read and write from about three or four years, but by early Victorian times a governess was employed. Among the middle class a common expedient was for children from several families to be assembled in the schoolroom of one household.

In *National Education: its Present State and Prospects* (1836), Frederic Hill put the case for middle-class infant schools. He argued that mothers should not be expected to devote all their time and attention to their young children, but that to leave them in the charge of servants led to their forming bad habits, whereas there would be social and educational advantages in sending them to infant school with other children of similar age and social standing. Authors of two articles in the Central Society of Education Papers for 1838 also made a similar plea for more infant schools for 'the wealthier classes of society' (Porter, 230; Fry, 243). A few such schools had come into existence by the late 1830s. There was one, charging an annual fee of £5, for pupils aged between two and eight in Stoke Newington, a residential district at a convenient commuting distance from the city of London (Porter, 1838, 230). Rowland Hill's famous 'progressive' school at Bruce Castle in Tottenham opened an infant section in 1836 for children aged four to nine (Fry, 1838, 244). There were also those opened by the early Pestalozzians.

The development of upper-middle-class suburbs was beginning to make private infant schools a viable economic proposition, especially when families tended to be larger as more children survived babyhood and women married young. These wealthier families were moving out of the towns to escape from the soot of factories and railways, the insanitary conditions which brought cholera and typhus, and the civil disturbances of bread riots and Chartism.

The social conditions were right but the demand for middle-class infant schools went largely unrealized until

29

the kindergarten movement of the 1850s. That this new and gentler theory of infant education won support must also be attributed to the changed attitude to early childhood that had come about by the second half of the century.

The romantic image

The change can be seen in the childrens' literature that was written. In the early decades of the century the consensus was that children's stories should not only entertain but convey a moral message and serve an instructional purpose: Thomas Day's *Sandford and Merton* (1789) had gone into nine editions by 1812, and Maria Edgeworth's collection of short stories, *The Parent's Assistant* (1798) remained very popular. Fairy stories were condemned until Mary Howitt's translations of Hans Andersen in 1846, which was followed by many other new collections as well as original works of fantasy in the decade 1849 to 1859. From the late 1830s children's stories were no longer dominated by morality, and from the early 1850s fictional children were not portrayed as sinners to be redeemed but as idealized paragons or as playful and adventurous. These changes in the style and content of children's literature were part of the wider romantic movement's reaction against rationalism and utilitarian philosophy.

The romantic image of early childhood was expressed by Wordsworth and Coleridge and developed further by the mid-century novelists. Wordsworth's nostalgia for childhood's spontaneous enthusiasm made a deep impression on the nineteenth-century attitude to children. Both he and Coleridge appealed for freedom for the child's imagination, and the latter saw the aim of education as the self-development of the innate self. In their general attitude to childhood and in their view of organic natural growth from infancy to maturity they contributed to the developmental approach and were echoed by Froebel. George Eliot's regret for the 'golden gates' of childhood and the idealized children of her earlier novels, which were published when Froebel's educational ideas were just becoming known in England, belonged to the same tradition. But Charles Dickens was the most influential in preparing the climate of opinion. 'Without Dickens the Victorian awareness would have been different; England would have felt differently ... and most surely differently about children' (Coveney, 1967, 119).

Though he later sentimentalized the image of childhood, in Nell of *The Old Curiosity Shop* (1841) and Paul of *Dombey and Son* (1848) he, like Charlotte Brontë in *Jane Eyre* (1847), drew attention to the lonely isolation of childhood and the psychology of children deprived of parental love. This, too, was an important feature of Froebel's child psychology.

Froebel's belief in the divinity of man was readily acceptable to English Protestantism of the mid-nineteenth century. A literary public that was soon to welcome the sentimentalism of Mrs Henry Wood's *East Lynne* (1861) found his romanticism compelling. As a consequence of the social demand for middle-class infant schools and the changed attitude to childhood, Froebelians, who came here after the prohibition of the Kindergarten in Prussia in 1851, found the English upper and middle classes were immediately interested in their methods of teaching young children.

Friedrich Froebel (1782-1852)

As a young schoolmaster Friedrich Froebel worked under Pestalozzi at Yverdun for two years. He then studied linguistics and natural science before returning to teaching at the age of thirty-four. It was at his school at Keilhau in Prussia, and later in Switzerland, that he began to evolve an educational theory which lead him to open the first kindergarten at Keilhau in 1837. There he worked out graduated exercises based on children's games, designed a simple educational apparatus in the 'gifts' to enable children to learn elementary laws of physical science by experiment, and systematized a series of 'occupations' for developing motor dexterity. His earlier experience with children of regular school age, around nine and ten, had convinced him of the importance of early childhood for the formation of character and attitudes to learning.

He had been impressed by Pestalozzi's work, but became convinced of the need for a more systematic methodology and the unity of theory and practice in an educational philosophy. He returned to the first principles of Rousseau and Pestalozzi and developed them to the logical conclusion of child-centred education, but infused this with romanticism and mysticism. Moreover, he borrowed from various contemporary German idealist philosophers, particularly Schelling and Hegel, and made use of fashionable scientific theories.

These features and his complicated style of writing made him difficult to understand, even in the original German. His ideas reached the English public through his many followers and exponents, or in translations open to misinterpretation.

At the practical, pedagogical level Froebel reiterated Pestalozzi in insisting that words must be connected with real things that the child saw or touched. He took Pestalozzi's practical emphasis on the importance of language as a means to understanding and verbalization of concepts, but gave priority of purpose first to self-knowledge, second to knowledge of God, and third to knowledge of nature, these three forms of knowledge being philosophically one. Similarly, his practical emphasis on the importance of spontaneous play derived from a mystic notion of play as 'the highest level of child development'.

The purpose of education was to enable man to give expression to his inner, divine nature as that developed through each stage of childhood. This process of continuous development should be neither hurried nor restricted, but could be aided by symbols which would heighten perception. Education would thus enable men 'to achieve their purpose as rational beings' (Froebel, 1826).

The six gifts which he devised for very young children were intended not only as playthings but as symbols of the child's growing consciousness of the universe. 'The ball or sphere is a symbol of perfection ... it is the symbol of my fundamental spherical principles of education and life', he wrote in 1831. Gift I was a box of six 1½-inch worsted balls in the primary and secondary colours; gift II comprised a wooden ball, cylinder and cube of the same size; gift III was a 2-inch cube divided into eight 1-inch wooden cubes; and the remaining gifts were each made up of boxes of more cubes similarly divided into cubes, half-cubes, square rods, oblongs, solid triangles and four-sided prisms. The 'occupations' for slightly older infants included geometric design with coloured wooden squares and triangles, paper folding, cutting and weaving, stick laying and construction, curved designs with cotton threads, drawing on squared paper, sewing pictures and embroidery on perforated cards. Explaining the nature and purpose of his play materials in the kindergarten, Froebel wrote (Lilley, 1967, 98):

> They are a coherent system, starting at each stage from the simplest activity and progressing to the most diverse and complex manifestations of it ... They cover the whole field of intuitive and sensory instruction and lay the basis for all further teaching. They begin by establishing spatial relationships and proceed to sensory and language training.

Matching appropriate activities to each stage of the child's development was a basic precept. This required kindergarten teachers to understand Froebel's theories of child development and be thoroughly trained in the use of his gifts and occupations. The latter requirement was easier to effect than the former, and the practical result was often a routine orthodoxy. Froebel's most significant long-term contributions to theories of infant education were the importance he attributed to play and the mother–child relationship in the process of natural growth in childhood, and his idea that teachers should wait till the child felt a need to learn before teaching basic skills. The mother–child theme immediately appealed to the Victorian literary public of Dickens' era, and became the focus of English and American child psychology for a century. His over-statement of the young child's need for women teachers was unquestioningly accepted at a time when teaching was one of the few careers open to women, and thus helped to promulgate an idea that became entrenched.

Froebel publicized his ideas with missionary zeal in his writings and by lecture tours. After his death this work was carried on with equal enthusiasm by a group of disciples, among whom the Baroness von Marenholtz-Bülow was one of the most influential. She was a Hegelian and consequently emphasized Froebel's philosophical idealism and the universality of his laws of child development. Her commitment to his ideas led to a doctrinaire exposition of his kindergarten methods.

The kindergarten movement

The Baroness von Marenholtz-Bülow began her series of international lecture tours with a visit to London in the summer of 1854. The quality press, such as *The Times* and *Athenaeum*, published articles on the kindergarten, and the Baroness received many invitations to fashionable drawing-rooms. The first exposition of Froebel's ideas in English was a pamphlet by Bertha Ronge, published the same year; and in the following year she and her husband produced *A Practical Account of the Kindergarten*. An English translation of the Baroness's explanation of kindergarten theory, *Women's Educational Mission*, was also published in 1855. The Ronges had opened a kindergarten in fashionable Bloomsbury in 1851, but this was for the children of German liberals who had emigrated from Prussia after the failure of the 1848 revolution. Frederic Hill's sons were their first English pupils.

When the Society of Arts held an educational exhibition in London in July 1854, the Baroness arranged for the director of the Hamburg kindergarten training school to demonstrate Froebel's gifts and occupations. The Ronges' kindergarten was opened to visitors at the same time, and they became the agents for Froebelian apparatus. They also began to train English kindergarten teachers, helped by the director from Hamburg. One of their students opened the second London kindergarten three years later, and a third was established at about the same time in Kensington by Miss Doreck from Wurttemburg.

Manchester had also attracted German émigré families and was the next obvious centre from which to promote kindergartens. Miss Barton, an English lady trained by the Ronges, opened the first in 1857. The Ronges moved there in 1859 and, following their lectures, the Manchester Committee for the Extension of the Kindergarten System was formed. In 1860 they started a kindergarten in Leeds. Throughout the 1860s several more kindergartens were opened, and from then on the movement developed rapidly, particularly in Manchester.

The pioneers of girls' education became associated with the kindergarten movement. The Home and Colonial Infant School Society established the Mayo High School as an offshoot of its work in training infant teachers in 1863, and eleven years later this, together with the Kindergarten and Non-Government Training College for secondary teachers, was transferred to Highbury Hill House where it eventually became the Highbury Hill High School. Miss Beale added a kindergarten to Cheltenham Ladies' College in 1876, and both North London Collegiate and Notting Hill High School introduced Froebelian methods into their preparatory departments for young children. All the schools of the Girls' Public Day School Trust, founded in 1873, eventually included kindergartens. The concurrent development of girls' secondary education was an important contributory factor in solving the previous problem of the shortage of suitable young women who could be trained as teachers for middle-class infant schools.

Kindergarten teachers and governesses

At first most of the kindergarten teachers came from Germany, but steps were taken to train English teachers in Froebelian methods. The Home and Colonial Infant School Society had developed a second department for training governesses from 1846, in addition to the original institution which trained infant teachers for the Voluntary Societies' elementary schools. In 1857 Heinrich Hoffman left his post as director of kindergarten training in Hamburg, and took up a new appointment with the Society to introduce Froebelian methods in both departments. The original Pestalozzian training programme was thus remodelled along Froebelian principles. The Manchester Kindergarten Training College was established in 1872, and two years later the British and Foreign School Society added a kindergarten training department to their Stockwell College. In the 1880s two more training centres were founded, the Froebel College at Bedford and the Skinner Street Training College which later became the Maria Grey College.

The promoters of the kindergarten movement were not only tireless enthusiasts, they were also efficient organizers able to win the support of influential business men with capital. These included the Manchester business man Sir William Mather, the Montefiore and the Rothschild families. That personalities among the English and European titled aristocracy were associated with the movement lent glamour and prestige, which helped when fund-raising was required.

Uniformity of standards and co-ordination of publicity were assured by the formation, in 1875, of the 'Froebel Society for the Promotion of the Kindergarten System', which began awarding its certificate the following July on the result of written and practical examinations, and later kept a register of approved kindergartens. In the next decade the Society started its own journal and, combining with the Manchester Kindergarten Association and various other local Kindergarten Companies, formed the National Froebel Union. The culmination of the Froebel movement's activities in the nineteenth century was the founding in 1894 of the Froebel Educational Institute for training teachers at a new college in West Kensington. This was originally an ambitious scheme for a training college with two model kindergartens and schools for children from three to fifteen, one to be fee-paying and the other free for working-class children. However, the subscription fund opened in 1892 with a target of £25,000 did not raise sufficient capital for the whole undertaking. Interviewed by the *Westminster Gazette* in 1894, Mr Claude Montefiore explained that the training college had been built first, the fee-paying model school and kindergarten was under construction, but that plans for the free kindergarten had been postponed until the sponsors had cleared their debts.

An off-shoot of the kindergarten movement was 'The Norland Institute for the Training of Ladies as Children's Nurses for Young Children', opened in 1892. The course was largely practical including story-telling, kindergarten

songs and games, some of the simpler kindergarten 'occupations', child care and hygiene. A similar course was run
at Sesame House in Hampstead from 1899.

A new attitude

By late Victorian times upper- and middle-class parents
could choose to employ Froebel-trained nursery nurses and
governesses. Those who lived in the larger residential
suburbs and fashionable towns were likely to have the
option, for about £5 a term, of sending their three- to
six-year-olds to a private kindergarten or the kindergarten
department of a girls' school. The junior departments of
many of these also took boys up to the age of seven or
eight, which was becoming the normal age for starting at
a boys' preparatory school. Through improved living conditions and medicine, children of the upper middle classes
now had a much better chance of survival. Parents consequently considered early education more seriously and
compassionately, as they became more emotionally involved with their young.

A master at a boys' preparatory school, writing in
Longman's Magazine, described the changed attitude to
education among the upper and middle classes: 'For we
are no longer of the same mind as our parents who sent
their children straight to a public school from the nursery.
Rather we consider that the child's life, from the age when
he fumbles with block letters, should be a continual and
graduated training for more advanced education to follow'
(Parker, 1898, 330-46). Preparatory school had become a
necessary stage in middle-class education for boys. Parents
expected them to provide high standards of instruction and
had also learnt to require kindness and pastoral care—
'coddling' as this master complained—and 'opportunities
of home life and surroundings' for the youngest. In *The
Education of Man* (1826) Froebel had written: 'To-day the

most urgent need in education is that the school should be united with the life of home and family.' This was realized, at least in part, among the upper and middle classes in late Victorian England whose attitude to young children had been considerably, if often unconsciously, influenced by Froebel's ideas.

4

The school board era:
1870-1902

The 1870 Education Act

There was some debate in both houses of Parliament in
the summer of 1870 concerning the minimum age at which
school boards should be permitted to make attendance
compulsory by bye-law. It was argued 'that five was too
tender an age for compulsory attendance' and 'that parents
would like to keep their children at home till they were
six years of age' (NEU, 1870, 441). Contrary arguments
were that children were safer at school than at home
and that 'it was never too early to inculcate habits of
decency, cleanliness and order. Besides, children thus
brought up learned more rapidly than those who had
passed their time in the gutter. The difficulty was to
obtain time for education without trenching on the time
for gaining a living ... beginning early and ending early
would present a solution' (ibid., 442). The latter arguments
prevailed and Clause 74(1) specified 'not less than five
years'. This broke with the original practice of the Volun-

tary Society schools which had regarded seven as the starting age, and thus the Act formally included the upper infant stage within elementary education. On this point Britain's policy became distinct from that of Europe and America.

The Code of 1871, which replaced the 1862 Code, divided the elementary course into six new Standards each defining the year's study in the three Rs between the ages of seven and thirteen. Thus the combined effect of the Act and the new Code was to create an infant stage below Standard I for the five to seven age range. But, as we have noted, there were already large numbers of children aged two or three to six attending the existing elementary schools. G. C. T. Bartley, who had access to official returns through his position at the Science and Art Department, made an independent survey of school provision in 1870. He estimated that three- to six-year-olds accounted for a third of all children then attending school. He also observed that the usual practice was to form two classes of children under seven: the babies' class comprised those under five whose curriculum consisted of learning to speak clearly, to understand pictures, to recite the alphabet and to march to music; the infant class of five- to seven-year-olds followed a curriculum based on the three Rs, simple manual tasks and sewing. In terms of age divisions, therefore, a nursery and an infant stage were already defined by 1871.

In introducing the Bill, W. E. Forster estimated that only 41 per cent of working-class children aged between six and ten attended grant-aided elementary schools (NEU, 1870, 6). The Act therefore aimed to secure 'efficient and suitable provision' (Clause 5) for the remaining 59 per cent and for the higher percentage under six and over ten for whom there was inadequate provision. This was very largely achieved in the course of the decade, particularly after the 1876 Act enforced compulsory attendance by means of bye-laws and school attendance orders.

41

By 1900 82·5 per cent of all children aged 'five and under fourteen' were attending grant-aided schools (Cd. 8244, 1950, 247), the short-fall being explained mainly by exemptions for senior pupils who passed Standard V.

Under-fives in elementary schools

As the majority of children over five years were gradually compelled to attend school so, for the reasons given in chapter 2, the number in attendance under five increased at roughly the same rate. Dame schools gradually disappeared as these children were accommodated in babies' classes of elementary and infant schools: there were over nineteen thousand under three years old in these classes during the mid 1870s (see Table 1).

TABLE 1   Infants aged three to five attending elementary schools in England and Wales (expressed as percentage of age group)

	1870	24·2
	1880	29·3
	1890	33·2
	1900	43·1

Source: Hadow, 1933, 29.

An increase of nearly 5 per cent occurred during the decade in which compulsion was introduced. The abolition of fees from 1891 clearly explains the remarkable increase of nearly 10 per cent in the last decade of the century, even though not all fees were immediately abolished. It seems likely that the steady increase from 1870 to 1890 of 4 to 5 per cent per decade in the voluntary attendance of infants under five reflects the willingness of skilled workers to use the elementary schools as public nurseries. The success of school boards in satisfying demand was even more remarkable than these percentages indicate as total numbers of children aged three to five rose from 1,179,228 in

1870 to 1,428,597 in 1900, while the total school population increased nearly threefold, and the number of three- to five-year-olds in school more than doubled.

During these years the purchasing power of workers in the skilled trades rose fairly steadily, as they were generally least liable to unemployment even during the depression of 1875 to 1880 and falling prices safeguarded the value of the wage increases their unions had previously won. Moreover, the growth of trade unions in the skilled trades meant that standard rates were won for a wider range of skilled workers. By the time that some industrial wages began to fall, as in the textile industries from the mid 1890s, school fees had been largely abolished. Evidently the lower paid, semi-skilled workers then also found it convenient to send their children to school below the statutory age. Until the Act of 1891 it had naturally been difficult to compel the attendance of children of the poorly paid, casually employed and unemployed, even though fees could be remitted in cases of proven necessity (Rubinstein, 1969). Nationally the percentage in average attendance of children on the school registers rose from 77·4 in 1890 to 81·6 in 1895 (Special Reports, 1897, 51).

As the children of statutory age among the unskilled working class were brought into school in the final decade of the century, so their younger brothers and sisters began to crowd into the babies' classes. At some schools the influx was so great that the head had to seek the school board's permission to exclude some of the youngest as a temporary measure (Log Book, 1899), and numbers of children under three declined nationally to three and a half thousand by the mid 1890s.

Though the process was slowest in the poorest neighbourhoods, where statutory attendance was lowest, the general pattern is clear. As school boards were established, attendance over five made compulsory and fees abolished, so infants of the manual working classes went to school

43

in increasing numbers below the statutory age, just as those of the more prosperous, skilled workers had even before 1870. Bartley, who was particularly concerned about lack of schools for the poorest children, had concluded 'that increased infant school accommodation must form one of the main features in practically carrying out any improved educational measure, more particularly applicable to populous districts' (1871, 115). In the last quarter of the century school boards and managers were forced by pressure of numbers, but not by direct legislation, to provide that increased accommodation. Indeed, many accepted this responsibility from the start and included a proportion of under-fives in their calculations for new school places required.

The need for nurseries

Nursery accommodation was what was really needed for the youngest of these children, but a babies' classroom was what was provided. There they were often penned into their seats to keep them from mischief (Miller, 1944). Continually rising numbers meant permanent overcrowding, even when school boards were building fast. A typical example was in Leicester where a new infant building was added to an elementary school in 1893, but the baby room which had been planned for forty was accommodating an average of eighty only five years later (Log Book, 1898).

Soon after 1870 members of the Charity Organisation Society in London were considering whether provision of public nurseries might be expedient. There were already a few cheap nurseries in east and central London but, with one exception in Stepney, they catered for the better paid section of the working class. These nurseries charged a daily fee of twopence to fourpence a child, accommodated about twenty children each, and were in the charge of a matron with a young girl assistant whose weekly wages

44

were respectively ten shillings and five shillings. W. G.
Howgraves reported to the Society that none of these
nurseries was financially self-supporting even though most
were rent-free: he calculated that they would need to
charge fivepence a day for a minimum of twenty children
to cover expenses including one meal but excluding rent
(*Charity Organisation Reporter*, 1872). Clearly these nurseries were beyond the means of even average wage
earners. Two free kindergartens had been opened in 1871
in the Manchester area, but were the only examples of
their kind before 1900.

The Charity Organisation Society, after investigating
fourteen nurseries, sent a report to the London School
Board recommending 'the School Board to attach to each of
its schools a room, either in the same building or otherwise, for the reception of infants', as this seemed the only
way of enabling parents to spare older children from
baby-minding at home (*Charity Organisation Reporter,*
1872). This plan was not accepted; but in practice London
and other urban school boards were compelled by circumstances to provide for large numbers of children from
upwards of two years old in their infant departments. The
London School Board sent a delegate to visit Sir William
Mather's two free kindergartens in Salford, and at the end
of the century opened four free nurseries; but this was
the only initiative by a public authority in the Victorian
era (Hewitt, 1958).

Kindergarten in infant schools

It might be expected that separate infants schools and
departments for children aged two to five would have
provided the opportunity for the introduction of Froebelian kindergarten principles into infant education for
the working classes. The Rev. M. Mitchell, HMI for Church
Schools in the Eastern Counties, hoped so after he had

45

seen Hoffman demonstrating kindergarten materials at the 1854 educational exhibition (Minutes, 1854-5). But several factors militated against this. Classes were far too large for the individual approach of the kindergarten, and there was such an acute shortage of qualified teachers that a babies' class of fifty to sixty was often left in charge of a girl of thirteen or fourteen years (Bailey, 1876). The kindergarten system was expensive in materials too. Pressure to begin teaching the three Rs as early as possible was one of the effects of the system of payment by results.

The requirements of the Standard I examination did not accord with Froebel's approach to learning mathematics as 'the expression of spatial conditions and properties', nor to his belief that 'the need to read and write must exist, and the urge, even the compulsion, to do so be unequivocally shown' before the child should be taught these skills. In the large, crowded baby and infant classes under an uncertificated or pupil–teacher, it was impossible to create the environment in which working-class children from illiterate homes could gradually be led to want to express themselves in writing, or be given opportunity to experiment freely with a range of art forms. Nor would this have been considered appropriate for children of 'the lower orders'.

The system of 'Standards' and 'payment by results' was intended to promote efficiency and economy in the elementary education of the working classes. Although it was not the government's intention to educate children under five, it was determined to produce mass literacy and numeracy at a level of competence represented by Standard IV at least; and it was clear from the debate on the 1879 Act that this might have to be achieved by the age of ten in many cases (NEU, 1870). In these circumstances Froebel's theories and the developmental tradition were inapplicable, not only in method but also in intention.

The propaganda of the Froebelians from 1854 neverthe-

less attracted considerable attention among those responsible for elementary education. At first the Home and
Colonial Infant School Society and the British and Foreign
School Society were the most influential bodies in introducing kindergarten techniques into infant schools. The former
remodelled its infant training course along Froebelian lines
from 1857; the latter Society was training infant teachers
in kindergarten methods from 1865 at Stockwell, and
from 1884 at its new Saffron Walden college.

These efforts to adapt the kindergarten to mass infant
education inevitably resulted in distortion of Froebel's pre-
cepts: whole classes of sixty or more simultaneously per-
formed a series of exercises with wooden blocks, beads
or sticks. Class instruction was substituted for individual
learning related to the child's stage of development. By the
1890s most of the school boards required these kindergarten
activities in their infant schools and classes.

The London School Board's original Regulations for Infant Schools required 'some such exercise of the hands and
eyes as is given in the "Kinder-Garten" system' (Robson,
1877, App. C). In 1874 the Board appointed a Froebelian,
Miss Bishop, to lecture on the kindergarten to its infant
teachers. But so long as the Code remained in force there
was little opportunity for any effective kindergarten work
in the schools, though in his General Report for 1882
Matthew Arnold commented favourably on the value of
'kindergarten exercises' in introducing 'creative activity
to relieve the passive reception of knowledge' (Marvin,
1908). The Education Department's circular to inspectors
in 1881 warned them of the debased form of kindergarten:
'It should be borne in mind that it is of little service to
adopt the gifts and mechanical occupations of the kindergarten unless they are so used as to furnish real training
in accuracy of hand and eye, in intelligence and obedience.'

This 'hand and eye' kindergarten training was seen as a
useful beginning by those who campaigned for manual

47

training in the elementary school as the necessary preliminary to better technical education for the future artisan.
W. Hewitt, for instance, regretted that these kindergarten
exercises were not carried on 'in a more advanced form,
with the children after they had left the infant schools'
(quoted by Selleck, 1968, 110). A leading Froebelian, Mrs
Schwabe, wrote in *Queen* in 1892 that 'the kindergarten
is the cradle of the technical school'.

The Froebel Society became concerned at the abuse of
the kindergarten system in elementary schools and, from
the time of Mundella's appointment as Vice-President of the
Education Department, began to influence official policy.
Circular 322 addressed to H.M. Inspectors in 1893 was a
long and detailed document on the instruction of infants
in Froebelian theory and practice, with a guide to what
children aged three to five and five to seven could do. The
Society presented evidence to the Cross Commission in
1886 on infant school buildings, qualifications for infant
teachers, and the case against an examination in reading
below Standard I. The 1892 Code recognized the Froebel
Certificate as a qualification for a post as assistant mistress
in an infant school.

By the 1890s the training and supply of teachers had
improved and the efficacy of the payment by results system
was being questioned in official circles. Infant departments
had grown to such a size that, as in Leicester, they accounted for one-third to one-half of the total average attendance
at elementary schools. When inspection replaced examination for the top infant classes in 1894, and for all Standards
the following year, some obstacles were removed from
the way to more enlightened nursery and infant teaching.

However, many factors hindered progress. Infant and
baby classes were still three times the size of Froebel's
recommended maximum of twenty-four for a kindergarten
class, and infant classrooms were all equipped with the
fixed, tiered gallery that had been recommended by Wil-

48

derspin and Stow early in the century. A generation of teachers had learned their trade under the discipline of payment by results, and nearly half the certificated teachers had never been trained but had become certificated by examination. In these circumstances Pestalozzian 'object lessons' and Froebelian 'kindergarten exercises' had become stereotyped, set pieces in the infant curriculum. Seated in the gallery the whole class did mechanical exercises with the 'gifts' at the teacher's instructions. Pressure to teach facts and the basic skills of reading, writing and arithmetic from an early age remained so long as children could legally begin employment at ten till 1893, and thereafter at eleven until the 1918 Act established a national statutory school leaving age of fourteen.

Mass infant education

The educational needs of working-class infants, for whom school ended in middle childhood, were more immediately utilitarian than those of upper- and middle-class kindergarteners who proceeded through preparatory school and a secondary education. Those responsible for public education were not concerned with the development of rational human beings but with ensuring a literate proletariat. Infant schools and classes had to provide a pre-elementary training for children whose parents might be illiterate, and whose homes could seldom provide much encouragement or intellectual stimulus. The large numbers of two-, three- and four-year-olds were in school because of the lack of public nurseries when most working-class women were in full-time employment. By accommodating these young children in babies' classes school boards reduced the demand for child-minders and thereby ended the scandal of dame schools (Hadow, 1933, 21); see Table 2.

The highest number of children under three attending school was recorded in 1875; thereafter their numbers

49

TABLE 2   Nursery–infant provision in elementary schools

Year	Under 3	3 to 4	4 to 5	5 to 6	6 to 7	Total of all ages in school
1871	6,687	111,397	164,211	196,999	207,930	1,802,419
1872	18,755	86,520	182,359	219,867	236,535	1,968,888
1875	19,358	111,409	232,630	297,134	323,464	2,744,300
1881	11,629	117,250	273,244	398,633	467,494	4,045,362
1885	8,986	127,540	290,181	441,038	503,000	4,412,148
1891	5,548	134,652	322,355	494,880	564,918	4,824,683
1895	3,508	165,175	362,539	534,986	587,579	5,299,469

Source: Special Reports, 1897, 51.

dropped steadily. The decrease may have been a result of pressure on accommodation as increased numbers of children over ten attended following the Acts of 1876, 1880 and 1891 and the raising of the minimum leaving age to eleven in 1893: the percentage of children over ten in the total school population rose from 29·13 in 1875 to 35·27 in 1895, while numbers of even older children in attendance also increased. Among children aged three to five both absolute numbers and the percentage of the age group in attendance continued to rise throughout the school board period. Infant education from three to seven was recognized in practice by the public, teachers and the inspectorate as the first stage in elementary education.

Educational theorists believed that the youngest children should be at home with their mothers: both Pestalozzi and Froebel had much to say on the nature and importance of early upbringing at home. But both the principle and the details were unrealistic in the slums. Though Pestalozzi and Froebel thought their infant pedagogy was applicable to all social classes, and Froebel envisaged the kindergarten as the initial stage in a national system of public education, neither had to face up to the exigencies of mass infant education in the conditions prevailing in industrial towns. Teachers with experience of these realities did not begin to develop an appropriate theory of infant education until the next century.

Part Two

The Twentieth Century

5

The rise of the nursery school: 1900-39

Recognition of the social need for nurseries came early in the twentieth century, but provision to meet that need was slow and depended largely on voluntary effort and agitation by dedicated pioneers. For the first quarter century social rescue and health considerations were the prime motives, until advances in child psychology began to show that nursery schools offered educational advantages. By mid-century nursery education was becoming accepted as desirable for a variety of reasons, for children of all social classes.

With the exception of the war years, which brought their own deprivations, the first third of the twentieth century was a period when the standard of living declined for most working-class families. Average real wages declined by about 10 per cent between 1899 and 1913 and barely recovered their position relative to the cost of living by the later 1930s. Unemployment, which included much intermittent as well as regional long-term unemployment, was the highest yet recorded between 1920 and World War II, and in the worst years of the world economic crisis in the early 1930s reached nearly three million or over 21 per cent. That fewer married women and widows were working must have further reduced the family standard of living. Moreover working-class families were still large as the trend to planned family limitation did not begin to spread among them till after World War I. Social welfare was only beginning to be a concern of government and was subject to cuts at times of economic stress.

Differences in living standards among the working class became more marked as the white-collar sector in the distributive trades, communications and commerce grew and people who found employment in these spheres were able to improve their circumstances. But for the depressed stratum in the slums of the big industrial towns the effects of poverty, overcrowding and malnutrition were cumulative for successive generations. In these districts the social and medical need for public nurseries and clinics was growing acute. Only the persistence of the extended family among the urban working class, and the likelihood that a grandmother or aunt lived near by, saved many from extremes of neglect and deprivation in the densely populated urban areas.

The mainstream of the organized labour movement was slow to take up the cause of nursery education, being more pre-occupied with opening opportunities for secondary. The Independent Labour Party, concerned about young children's health, campaigned for clinics and school medical inspection. A Fabian *Tract* of 1891, drafted by Sidney Webb, suggested that school boards provide crêches and kindergartens, and later *Tracts* in the early 1900s continually urged the need for nurseries and clinics. Then in 1926 the Bradford Independent Labour Party appointed a commission to prepare a report on the socialist conception of education. Part I of this report was devoted to the nursery school and recommended 'the setting up of nursery schools for all children from two to seven years of age, and the progressive disappearance, as they are set up, of infant departments'. In their perspective of nursery education as integral to the whole educational continuum of the common school, the ILP was in direct line with the Owenites a hundred years before but several decades in advance of majority opinion.

Free kindergartens

Just as elementary education had initially been provided by voluntary, philanthropic effort in the early nineteenth century, so nursery education had similar origins in the twentieth century. Leading figures in the Froebel movement in Britain were the first to provide free nursery education for children aged three to six years in working-class districts. In 1871, nearly thirty years before Froebel organizations became active in this field, Sir William Mather opened the Salford Day Nursery which employed a kindergarten teacher from Germany, and a year afterwards founded a free kindergarten at Pendelton. Twenty years later he was chairman of the committee formed to raise capital for the Froebel Educational Institute. When they failed to collect enough subscribed capital the committee abandoned their project for a free kindergarten alongside the training college and middle-class kindergarten and school for fee-payers. Financial problems beset the Froebelians' early attempts to start free kindergartens. The first free kindergarten in London was opened at Woolwich in 1900 by Adelaide Wragge, principal of the Blackheath Kindergarten Training College, but was closed through lack of money. Then the Michaelis Guild raised funds to aid two successful ventures in Blackheath and at the Maurice Hostel Settlement in Hoxton; and in 1908 the Michaelis Free Kindergarten was opened at Notting Hill, followed two years later by the Somers Town Nursery School in St Pancras. Manchester Froebelians opened another free kindergarten in Salford in 1908, and Reid's Court Free Kindergarten opened in Edinburgh in 1903.

Esther Lawrence, who became principal of the Froebel Educational Institute (FEI) in 1901, claimed in a pamphlet published in 1912 that the Froebel movement was active 'in most poverty-stricken and deprived districts of large towns' including two or three in Edinburgh. Though their contribution was numerically small, free kindergartens began to be successfully established for three- to six-year-olds in working-class districts just at the time when elementary schools were excluding children under five; they were the first example of separate free nursery schools in Britain. They continued to depend on subscriptions and donations until they became eligible for grant as nursery schools in 1919.

Working with slum children was new for the Froebelians: Esther Lawrence commented on 'the type and poverty of their experience', but noticed how much more capable they were of looking after themselves compared with middle-class kindergartners. An early pamphlet, entitled *Objects of the Michaelis Free Kindergarten*, emphasized training 'in habits of cleanliness' and 'the progress of morality, order and freedom'. Froebelian principles had to be pragmatically re-interpreted in these new circumstances, though there was some American experience to draw on. The usual activities included handicrafts based on Froebelian 'occupations', singing and dancing, stories and nursery rhymes, imaginative play with dolls and dolls' houses, and domestic training. Provision of baths was often necessary, a midday sleep on hammocks or cots was required, and a doctor paid a weekly visit. Emilie Michaelis, the first principal of the FEI, distinguished nursery schools from infant schools by their provision for movement and free play, absence of formal instruction and opportunity for individual care and attention. They were undoubtedly healthy and happy places for the few three- to six-year-old slum children lucky enough to attend them.

Maria Montessori (1870-1952)

When the Froebelians were opening free kindergartens in Britain, Dr Maria Montessori was experimenting with a new form of pre-school education at her Casa dei Bambini in a tenement in Rome, as part of the remodelling of slum housing by the Association of Good Building. There she adapted apparatus she had originally designed for use with mentally deficient children, based on the theory and practice of Itard and Séguin in their work with the subnormal. She approached the problems of deprived children from the standpoint of doctor and psychologist, and applied her scientific training to the observation of these very young children of the slums. From her observations she evolved a theory of consecutive stages of mental development in which she postulated significant periods for specific aspects. She found that development of the five senses, particularly sight and touch, was fundamental to intellectual growth and understanding concepts of abstract qualities. Accordingly, she designed didactic materials to promote sensory development through exploiting the young child's delight in repeating the same task. In this way she devised 'the prepared environment' of the nursery school where children aged three to seven learnt to choose appropriate materials and, indeed, showed preference for her materials over mere toys. It was a structured environment in which she claimed that children learnt to enjoy learning and helping one another.

Order was essential if the children were to profit from this 'prepared environment' in which 'auto-education' or individual learning replaced the classroom instruction of the traditional infant school. But it was order based on 'active discipline', by which she meant self-discipline, not repressive discipline which she condemned as destroying individuality. To this end prizes and punishment were abandoned, and rooms furnished with light tables and chairs including little wicker armchairs. Each Casa dei Bambini was fitted out as a child-sized world.

Careful attention was given to physical development and detailed records kept for each child. With the youngest there were exercises to foster sensory-motor development correct breathing and speech, and learning how to dress and wash themselves. Montessori used some of Froebel's exercises such as paper-folding and clay modelling, but rejected others as unsuited to a young child's eye and hand co-ordination. Education of the senses was, however, the central feature for which she developed didactic material such as graduated rods and cylinders, geometric insets, colour tablets and so on. This material was intended to be almost teacher-proof and self-corrective: 'Not upon the ability of the teacher does such education rest, but upon the didactic system. This presents objects which, first, attract the spontaneous attention of the child, and, second, contain a rational graduation of stimuli' (Montessori, 1964 ed., 174-5). In applying the method the Montessori teacher was required to guide but not force the child, to direct but not instruct. Naming of objects and qualities was a key feature of the Montessori method, and many didactic games centred on this. Detailed accounts were given in chapters 12 to 15 of *The Montessori Method*, published in 1912.

Initially Montessori accepted that reading and writing should be postponed to at least six years, but she found that many four-year-olds were ready to proceed from pre-writing motor exercises to the skill of writing. Her significant new pedagogical principle was the separation of writing and reading as two distinct skills, the former largely mechanical and the latter 'an abstract intellectual culture, which is the interpretation of ideas from graphic symbols, and is only acquired later on' (Montessori, 1964 ed., 267). Sandpaper letters enabled the children to learn the shapes by both sight and touch, the latter familiarizing them with the movement required to reproduce the shape. Composition of phrases and sentences by the children themselves was found to be a necessary stage that established 'logical language' before proceeding to reading with understanding rather than merely mechanical reading. The sequence of this system for teaching writing and reading was described in detail in chapters 16 to 17 in *The Montessori Method*.

Montessori's ideas and materials soon became known in England, and from 1919 to 1938 a six-month training course for teachers was run in London every alternate year. The Froebelians reacted to her theory and practice with closed minds and continuously accused her of rigid formality, mere sense-training and neglect of the child's imagination. Her apparent mistrust of teachers' ability to use their initiative aroused the suspicions of Froebelians who were themselves fighting against the mechanical use of kindergarten exercises in babies' and infants' classes. Nor did they accept her rejection of fantasy as escapism, and her insistence that imaginative play and stories must be firmly based on reality.

This hostility prevented Montessori's ideas from having much direct and immediate influence in Britain, despite the fact that she had systematically developed them in a context similar to the slum conditions where a new type of nursery education was urgently needed. The Froebelians were entrenched in the English educational world as the experts on the education of young children, acknowledged alike by government, training colleges and public opinion. The reaction against formal instruction for children under five in elementary schools gave credence to their condemnation of Montessori's more positive methodology and didactic materials, especially as these were often interpreted by her disciples in a stereotyped and routine manner. Moreover, her methods did not accord with the prevalent notion of nursery schools for the industrial poor as little more than pre-school welfare centres. The sequential continuity of her methods for three- to seven-year-olds was at variance with the sharp distinction currently being made in the state system of education between children under and over five. When money for state infant schools was scarce and free kindergartens depended on donations, the expense of Montessori apparatus was a further deterrent.

At the time her influence was largely indirect, except in the establishment of some private Montessori schools for young children in middle-class districts; the early acquisition of the literary skills was considered an advantage in middle-class circles, where no significance was attached to the age of five. The principles of the prepared environment and the materials she used strongly influenced the design of educational toys provided in most nursery schools, both public and private. Margaret McMillan and Susan Isaacs selected what they found useful in her methods and materials, while rejecting her extreme didacticism, and followed her in recognizing the importance of the individual child's development. In recent years American educationists concerned with developing pre-school programmes for underprivileged children in downtown districts have revived interest in Montessori methods, and have re-published her writings.

Margaret McMillan (1860-1931)

The pioneer in the creation of the English nursery school was Margaret McMillan. She came to this work through socialism and socio-medical welfare. From campaigning with the Independent Labour Party in Bradford in the

1890s against the half-time system and for medical inspection in elementary schools and the corollary of clinics to provide treatment, she went to London where she joined the Froebel Society, worked with the Workers' Educational Association and was elected to the National Administrative Council of the Independent Labour Party. She had seen the effects of industrial and rural poverty in Bradford and the villages of Kent before working with the ILP in the East End of London, and she understood that social welfare required political action. She and her sister, Rachel, determined to persuade the Board of Education to tackle the inherent health problems through school clinics. Supported by funds from an American millionaire, the approval of the Board of Education and facilities provided by the London County Council, they opened an experimental clinic at Bow in 1908. Two years later this was transferred to Deptford as the Deptford Schools Treatment Centre, serving 6,000 children a year. From this they developed their night camps which, in turn, inspired them to run an open-air nursery school in 1913. Their insistence on open-air provision, with shelters open on one side, was because tuberculosis, eye, ear and respiratory complaints were endemic among slum children at that time, and the spread of epidemics was a serious hazard.

Her practical starting-point was health rescue from the damaging effects of slum homes, but this immediately led to educational implications in which Séguin's work with defectives was relevant. For she found that 'subnormal traits of many orders have their starting-point here' (McMillan, 1923, 23) in nasal complaints that prevented children from learning to speak properly, early deformity at two or three 'through having been obliged to sit all day with their legs tucked under a table' (ibid, 34) and fingers almost atrophied because they never had an opportunity to use them. Consequently, she came to the conclusion that 'To educate the hand and to safeguard the speech impulse:

that is perhaps the main work—of a formal kind—of the nursery school. When that work is well done there will be a new science of pedagogy and the present dry results of (mental) classification will be out of date' (ibid, 23). Experience had shown her that the so-called intelligence tests, currently used for classification rather than diagnosis, judged children's actual performance which inevitably reflected their stultifying home background: consequently these tests categorized many slum children as mentally retarded or subnormal. Remedial training and the stimulating environment of the nursery school enabled many to overcome the inhibiting effects of early deprivation.

Remedial work apart, her socialist vision which inspired all her work meant that ultimately she wanted all children to develop their potential. She interpreted this largely in terms of creative imagination dependent upon sensory and emotional experience and satisfaction of 'the higher hungers' for aesthetic sensitivity. Some of her writing verges on mysticism, but she was a very practical person. Her contribution to primary education was to draw attention to the importance of aesthetics in the curriculum. In *Education Through the Imagination*, originally written in 1904, she expounded her educational philosophy in these terms, clearly reflecting the influence of William Morris and John Ruskin. Her arguments were primarily humanistic, but included recognition that twentieth-century technology required 'a new order of workman' capable of exercising 'enterprise, initiative—plus what is learned—Imagination' (1923, 11). The function of the nursery school was to further physical, emotional and mental well-being.

In practice she devoted much of her attention to preschool education, but she saw her principles as applicable to older children too. The nursery and nursery school merely made a right beginning possible. And, whereas the free kindergarten catered for children from three to six years, the McMillan nursery and nursery school took them from two to eight or nine, though most were between three and seven or eight years: it certainly encompassed the infant school, as did the Montessori Casa.

The slums were the context in which Margaret McMillan evolved her concept of the nursery school as an educational institution. Essentially an eclectic who was willing to adapt in the light of experience, she derived her educational ideas from Pestalozzi and Froebel as well as from Robert Owen and Marxism. Like Montessori, with whom she claimed to 'have nothing in common', she was also much influenced by Séguin's work with the mentally deficient. Although she disapproved of Montessori's insistence on a correct method-ology, she saw value in some of her materials and designed some of her own for developing colour perception.

In her nursery school she provided a child-sized world where young children could learn to undertake everyday domestic activities, have full scope for imaginative play and experiment while learning motor control and develop-ing their five senses under skilled guidance in a physically healthy environment. As she said, 'In the open-air nursery we have tried to plan his environment with a view to the young child's needs' (1923, 35). This planning involved abandoning classes in favour of small groups of six under-fives or twelve over-fives, with a young girl 'helper' for each group under the supervision of a trained teacher. She aimed at a less systematically structured learning en-vironment than Montessori, one that was more homely and hence provided many opportunities for informal learning as in a lively middle-class household. She once said: 'We must try to educate every child as if he were our own and just as we would educate our own.' This was the object of the McMillan nursery school, which was clearly in the Owenite developmental tradition.

Official policy 1902-29

The damage done by poverty and slums to the health of

the nation's manpower was brought to the government's notice when army medical officers examined recruits for service in the Boer War. Sir Frederick Maurice, Inspector-General of Recruiting, estimated that probably 60 per cent of men were unfit, and Parliament was informed of the rejection of thousands of potential army recruits. These revelations evoked such alarm that an Inter-Departmental Committee on Physical Deterioration was set up, and published its Report in 1904. Witnesses gave evidence that working mothers sent very young children to school to get them out of the way, and suggested that school attendance was responsible for physical deterioration when young children were forced to sit still and quiet on benches, doing work that was too fine and hence injured their eyesight. The Committee, though critical of physical conditions in many schools, stated categorically 'that the general effects of school life are not prejudicial to health' (Cd. 2175, 59). Several witnesses had urged the need for nurseries rather than schools for children aged three to five years, and the Committee went so far as to recommend the establishment of municipal crèches 'wherever it was thought desirable, owing to the employment of women in factories'.

In view of the many criticisms about under-fives in elementary schools, the Board of Education asked its women inspectors to report and advise on the matter. Their Report was published in 1905. Parts of it were so damning of certain schools that it was censored before publication.

These women inspectors were unanimous 'that the children between the ages of three and five get practically no intellectual advantage from school instruction', and claimed 'the evidence is very strong against attempts at formal instruction for any children under five' (Cd. 2726). While recognizing that for children from the worst slum homes it was better for their health and physique if they went to school, the Report advocated extensive provision of 'nursery schools rather than schools of instruction'. But there was as yet no clear idea about what nursery schools should be: they were envisaged as child-minding havens in the slums, fostering better health and developing good habits and some pre-schooling skills such as talking and manual dexterity. It was therefore suggested that the Board of Education should consider the whole question of the character and function of nursery schools.

The case for public provision of nursery schools in industrial towns was strong, if only on humanitarian grounds. But public elementary schools were under pressure from increasing numbers of full-time older pupils, especially since the 1893 School Attendance Act had raised the statutory age for total and partial exemption to eleven: some schools, where many had previously attended only on part-time shifts, had obtained permission in the late 1890s to exclude under-fives to make room. The elementary school population of statutory age was still rising, attendance was more effectively enforced, and in the years 1900 to 1903 the Board noted a marked increase in numbers over eleven years. These pressures came at a time when the recent high cost of the Boer War was still a factor in Treasury calculations. Abolition of grant for children under three soon led to their exclusion from school. The Board of Education responded to further pressures for economy and to the women inspectors' criticisms by adding the following clause to Article 53 of the 1905 *Code of Regulations for Public Elementary Schools*: 'Where the local education authority have so determined in the case of any school maintained by them, children who are under five years of age may be refused admission to that school' (Cd. 2579).

Neither money nor permission was given for alternative accommodation in nurseries. Three years later the Consultative Committee to the Board of Education, which had been asked to investigate 'School Attendance of Children Below the Age of Five', reported that of the 327 local education authorities, 32 had wholly excluded all children under five and a further 136 were excluding some, usually the youngest (Cd. 4259, 1908). The major industrial towns were not, on the whole, among the 32. This Committee argued the social need for nursery schools more strongly than the two previous Reports, and considered that none of the objections urged against school attendance under five years was sufficient to justify exclusion. It assumed that where home conditions were satisfactory a child under five should be at home with its mother, but recognizing the prevalence of unsatisfactory home circumstances in many industrial towns it recommended: 'In the greater part of most towns and urban areas the majority of children who will eventually attend an elementary school should be regarded as eligible for admission to nursery schools when they are three years old.'

This Report included detailed and enlightened guidance on premises, equipment, curriculum and staffing of nursery schools, and recommended that they should be firmly placed within the public educational system, attached to a public elementary school and under local education authority control. These recommendations were in advance of most contemporary opinion: the discretionary restrictions of the 1905 Code continued to be effective in a decade when total numbers in elementary schools rose by nearly a million and education estimates went up by almost four million pounds. Children under three ceased being admitted and numbers between three and five years were nearly halved.

TABLE 3   Nursery and infant age groups in elementary schools

	Under 3 years	3-5 years	5-7 years
1901	2,484	610,989	1,230,054
1903	1,460	608,389	1,249,057
1904	nil	583,268	1,263,147
1911	nil	332,888	1,295,894

Source: Board of Education, *Annual Report and Statistics 1912-13*

Despite mounting social and medical evidence of the urgent need for nursery schools—reports of the first medical inspections in 1908 showed that 40 per cent of five-year-old entrants needed medical attention—the 1918 Education Act failed to make statutory provision. Local education authorities were given discretionary permission to provide or aid nursery schools, for which grants might be made available by the Board of Education, but no real pressure was put on them. Twelve voluntary nursery schools already in existence were given grants, but only eight new maintained nursery schools were opened in the next three years. Two Circulars in 1921 and 1922 severely restricted expenditure and effectively prevented further action until they were withdrawn by the first Labour government in 1924. Even then there was little positive encouragement, and two years later the grant for children under five in infant schools was reduced. This stop-go policy made non-sense of the discretionary clause in the 1918 Act for nearly twenty years. By 1929 only a thousand more children were attending nursery schools than unaided voluntary effort had accommodated before the Act (see Table 4).

TABLE 4   *Maintained and aided nursery schools*

	Aided	Maintained	Total	Children
1919	12	1	13	288
1921	12	8	20	744
1927	15	12	27	1,160
1929	16	12	28	1,233

Source: Board of Education, *Annual Reports and Statistics*

Meanwhile the percentage of under-fives in elementary schools continued to decline (see Table 5)—a trend further encouraged by the reduction in grant from 1926 by *Circular* 1371.

TABLE 5   *Three- and four-year-olds in elementary schools* (as percentage of age group in England and Wales)

1900	43·1
1910	22·7
1920	15·3
1930	13·1

Source: Hadow, 1933, 29.

The nursery school was envisaged largely in terms of social and medical care, not as an educational institution. Medical officers and voluntary social workers were its main protagonists. It thus fell outside the mainstream of educational provision and was most vulnerable to pressures for economy. The parents whose children nursery schools would benefit were among the most inarticulate section of the population. When working mothers could not find places for their youngest children in babies' classes of elementary schools they had to resort to local child-minders, the twentieth-century descendants of the dame schools. State responsibility in social welfare was only beginning to be accepted with the introduction of school medical inspection in 1907, old age pensions in 1908 and a parsimonious national insurance scheme in 1911. The welfare of the under-fives was a low priority.

Susan Isaacs (1885-1948)

Meanwhile a new influence was at work on the concept of the nursery school, approaching its function from the standpoint of a more scientific study of the psychology of young children than had previously been attempted. The child study movement began in the 1890s when Mary Lynch formed the British Child Study Association and the Childhood Society was established to collect statistics on physical and mental development. This movement was set on a sound footing when Susan Isaacs began her work at the experimental Malting House School in 1924. There she and her assistants recorded systematic and detailed observations of a group of children aged between two-and-a-half and nine years, in the everyday situations of this small, private school where the children were free to follow their own interests and inclinations. The reason for this approach was explained by Evelyn Lawrence, later director of the National Froebel Foundation, when she joined the staff in 1927: 'an indispensable preliminary to improvement in education theory was a detailed and consistent study of a group of children living in conditions of maximum freedom' (Gardner, 1969, 60). Although many of these children were exceptionally bright—their IQ range was from 106 to over 140—many were emotionally disturbed. This method of research was applied by Susan Isaacs and her students in observations of more average children in nurseries and play centres, particularly while she was head of the new Child Development Department at the London Institute of Education for ten years from 1933, and in her study of evacuee children during World War II.

The Malting House School was also an educational venture where innovations could be tried out. Both Geoffrey Pyke, the financial wizard who founded the school, and Susan Isaacs clearly hoped to change current ideas and practice in the education of young children. Inadvertently and deliberately, the school attracted a lot of attention. Susan Isaacs' lectures and writings undoubtedly had a far reaching influence on the concept of the nursery school and the upbringing of young children. Her regular advice as 'Ursula Wise' in *The Nursery World* from 1929 to 1936 was especially influential in reaching a wide public, while her two major works, *Intellectual Growth in Young Children* (1930) and *Social Development in Young Children* (1933) based on observations of the Malting House children made a great impression on the educational world.

Her academic training enabled her to relate the findings

69

of recent psychology to her own systematic child observations and thus carry forward the theoretical basis of nursery education beyond the point reached by Margaret McMillan. That she had studied and experienced psychoanalysis was of significance in her observations and interpretations of children's early emotional behaviour: Sir Cyril Burt said that 'one of her chief contributions was an early and partial acceptance of the ideas about children *deduced* by Freud'. This was important for freeing nursery training from the moral obligation to inhibit sexual curiosity and for winning acceptance for a more generally permissive attitude to early upbringing and discipline. She thus brought rational judgment to support the hitherto rather sentimental reaction against repression and insistence on obedience for its own sake in the nursery years. Of great importance was her contribution to a scientific analysis of young children's intellectual growth and social development. The significance of individual differences in development that her observational method revealed led to an appreciation of the value of individual records in nursery and infant schools. Her rejection of the narrow behaviourist psychology that was then fashionable, and her emphasis on language and reasoning were of fundamental importance for the evolution of a sound pedagogical approach to nursery education.

Susan Isaacs re-established, but on a new basis and within the developmental tradition, the function of the nursery school in promoting intellectual growth. In this she had been influenced by Montessori, whose teaching materials and, to some extent, whose methodology were used at the Malting House. Her own brief contemporary description illustrates how she viewed the function of the nursery school (van der Eyken, 1969, 39):

The children are free to explore and experiment with the physical world, the way things are made, the fashion in which they break and burn, the properties of water and gas and electric light, the rain, sunshine, the mud and the frost. They are free to create either by fantasy in imaginative play or by real handling of clay and wood and bricks. The teacher is there to meet this free inquiry and activity by his skill in bringing together the material and the situations which may give children the means of answering their own questions about the world.

Middle-class nursery education

Nursery education as envisaged by Susan Isaacs would be advantageous for any pre-school child, regardless of home background. Bertrand Russell argued this cogently in *On Education Especially In Early Childhood*, which was popular enough to be reprinted eight times between 1926 and 1946. He concluded 'that even the best parents would do well to send their children to a suitable (nursery) school from the age of two onwards, at least for part of the day' (1946, 179).

Until after World War II few middle-class parents sent their children to a nursery school, though many started at about four in a kindergarten or preparatory department of a day school and others were taught by a governess. But, as those Cambridge parents who chose to send theirs to the Malting House School showed, some were beginning to recognize the possible advantages of a nursery school community for children who lacked the experience of growing up in a large family. Since the last decade of the nineteenth century the professional and employing classes had been restricting family size and seemed by the inter-war period to have settled for about two children, often with a gap of several years between them. Second-generation parents of small families could, from their own childhood experience, see some of the disadvantages that a good nursery school might offset.

Middle-class parents, moreover, were no longer content to leave their children to the care of an untrained nanny from the servant class but, from Edwardian times, were increasingly employing Norland-trained nursery nurses. Yet even this arrangement was proving disadvantageous for children over about three years. The experience of the Chelsea Open Air Nursery School, opened by four middle-class parents in 1928 and closed only at the outbreak of war, revealed a different kind of deprivation. It took months to train children who had had nannies to be independent in dressing, washing and use of the lavatory. Their teacher noticed that 'the children at this nursery school were more talkative than in slum nursery schools, but less interested in making use of the environment furnished' (Davies, 1940). They were accordingly nicknamed the 'Kensington Cripples'.

In 1930 the Annual Report of the NSA noted an 'increase in small private nursery schools, staffed by trained nursery school teachers and charging fees for attendance'. These were mostly Froebelian kindergartens or Montessori nursery schools, admitting children at three and four years old.

Early upbringing was beginning to be seen as a complex task in which a good nursery school had a part to play. This part was more obvious if the home circumstances were characterized by poverty and malnutrition; but there was a growing recognition that children might be emotionally crippled in materially poor or wealthy homes, and that many homes failed to provide sufficient intellectual stimulation to satisfy the natural curiosity and imagination of three- to five-year-olds. A city upbringing was regarded as particularly inhibiting: writing in 1926 Bertrand Russell advocated nursery schools 'at the very least, for all children who live in towns' (1946, 177).

The Consultative Committee Report (1933)

The new awareness that experiences during early childhood are important for subsequent development won official recognition when the Consultative Committee, which
had just completed its Report on *The Primary School* (1931)
was asked: 'To consider and report on the training and
teaching of children attending nursery schools and infants'
departments of public elementary schools, and the further
development of such educational provision for children
up to the age of 7+.'

The Report on *Infant and Nursery Schools*, published
in 1933, came out in favour of extensive provision of
separate nursery schools of the McMillan prototype in
urban working-class districts, while also accepting that
'there are areas in which nursery classes within infant
schools or departments will satisfy the existing need'.

Since the Consultative Committee's Report in 1908 there
had been considerable quantitative research by doctors and
psychologists on the development of young children and
the functioning of the central nervous system. The new
Committee supplemented evidence received for the 1931
report with further and detailed evidence concerning the
first seven years from Professor H. A. Harris of University
College Hospital on physical development, and from Professor Cyril Burt and Susan Isaacs on mental and emotional
development. The important second and third chapters
were based on these authoritative sources.

Reporting at a time when there was much concern
about malnutrition in early childhood, caused by ignorance
and poverty, the Committee drew attention to the role
of nursery schools in promoting health, educating parents
and providing opportunity for regular medical inspection.
'The nursery school is distinguished from the ordinary
school by the emphasis placed on physical well-being.'
But the Committee saw the nursery school as 'a desirable

73

adjunct to the national system of education' not only 'where housing and general economic conditions are seriously below average', but also in more favourable districts where model nursery schools would provide centres for studying problems of child development. A good home was still considered the best environment for children under five, but the value of nursery education in stimulating intellectual development was beginning to be recognized particularly for city children. 'In the ordinary urban environment there is little to satisfy the child's natural impulses: it is important, therefore, to provide an environment which will do so.' It was assumed that natural surroundings associated with country life were likely to foster natural development and should be imported into the city nursery school and playground.

The nursery school envisaged by the 1933 Report was modelled on experience of nursery education in those industrial towns where pioneering work was being done. Descriptions of some of these, such as the Rachel McMillan Nursery School at Deptford, the Froebelian Notting Hill Nursery School, a Bradford combined nursery–infant school and a nursery class at a Leicester infant school, were included in Appendix IV. The concept of nursery education derived from Owen and Pestalozzi, drew eclectically on the theory and practice of Froebel, Montessori, McMillan and Isaacs, and was strengthened by contemporary research on the physical, mental, emotional and social development of young children. Froebel's influence was strong in the importance attributed to play and to the 'spontaneous unfolding of the child's natural powers', and Montessori's in the emphasis on sensory training. The open-air type of school was favoured mainly because it lessened the chances of infection spreading.

By selectively drawing this heritage together in coherent recommendations the Report dealt a severe blow to some long-accepted psychological theories and many established

74

practices. Recognition of the influence of environment and early experiences called in question the extent of innate characteristics. Recognition of individual differences and the importance of allowing opportunity for spontaneity ran counter to mass instruction in babies' and infants' classes. Experimental research on vision showed that 'children under the age of seven should not be expected to read small print or indeed to do any close work for long periods', while tests indicated that their concentration span was short and rote learning inefficient. Knowledge about the development of the central nervous system and muscular control showed that 'fine work with hands and fingers should not be expected', but opportunity for running and climbing was essential.

The Report was a landmark in the theory of nursery education which it placed firmly in the developmental tradition. In the context of the time special emphasis was necessarily given to physical welfare, but the way was opened for a balanced approach to all aspects of the young child's development. The aim was 'to aid and supplement the natural growth of the normal child' in a planned yet unrestrictive educative environment, with opportunity for individual attention and informal work with small groups.

Campaign for nursery education

In the inter-war period the role of the progressive education movement and the political Labour movement was significant in the campaign for nursery education. The former's journal, *New Era*, supported the Nursery School Association and private progressive schools often admitted children of nursery school age. The freer ethos of the McMillan and Isaacs nursery school appealed to progressives who believed it would provide a sure foundation for mental health and hoped it would influence schools for

75

older children. *New Era* ran a special number on nursery education in 1938.

Within the labour movement the ILP consistently supported nursery schools for the poor from the days of the McMillan sisters' early campaigns. From the mid-1920s the Labour Party, TUC and WEA became committed to the idea that nursery education should be made available to all as a matter of social justice, and Ramsay MacDonald was himself a vice-president of the NSA. Bertrand Russell expressed the view of some socialists: 'The nursery school, if it became universal, could, in one generation, remove the profound differences in education which at present divide the classes' (1926, 181). Though successive Labour governments vacillated when confronted by economic crises, they remained sensitive to campaign pressures and the NSA's accusation of 'reactionary policy', and sanctioned expansion in 1924 and 1929.

All three political party manifestoes in 1935 promised more nursery schools. This was a measure of the success of a ten-year campaign by the NSA and the impact of the Consultative Committee's Report. The extension of the Hadow Committee's terms of reference to nursery education may be largely attributed to pressure by the NSA and the personal influence of key members.

People engaged in nursery and infant education and other enthusiastic protoganists had become convinced of the value of nursery education for children of all social classes. But they were divided about the respective merits of separate nursery schools or nursery classes in infant schools. Progressive infant teachers welcomed the child-centred influence of nursery education, while others valued the socialization and training that enabled five-year-olds to adjust more easily to formal teaching. The effectiveness of a campaign for universal nursery education was likely to hinge on a resolution of this controversy and a clarification of aims to convince the public and officialdom that

76

nursery education was an extension of nursery care and gave young children a richer experience than any home could offer alone. In the social conditions of the time attention was inevitably focused on remedial and health aspects of nurseries in the slums, where the need was obvious. Though there were signs that nursery education was beginning to be seen as generally worthwhile, there was little consensus on its purpose.

Limited expansion 1929-39

The McMillan Nursery School won official approval and was the prototype for the limited growth of nursery schools in the decade following World War I. The Nursery Schools Association was formed in 1923 with Margaret McMillan as president, to campaign for extensive provision of these nursery schools; and two years later the Labour Party and the Trade Union Congress issued a joint policy statement in favour of expansion of nursery schools and classes. But progress was slow. By 1928 thirteen nursery schools had been opened by local education authorities and fifteen run by voluntary bodies were receiving grants.

The distinction between nursery education and nursery care was recognized, though social rescue and physical welfare remained important motives. During World War I, when the number of officially sponsored public nurseries reached 175, the aim had been to release women for work in munition factories while providing day care for their pre-school children where social need was greatest. Most of these nurseries were closed down after the war. When limited expansion became possible it was in the form of nursery schools and classes.

Under the new Labour government the Ministry of Health and the Board of Education issued a joint Circular in 1929 urging local authorities to provide open-air nursery schools, day nurseries or nursery classes attached to infant schools. This had immediate effect for local authorities opened a further nine nursery schools within a year, and by March 1931 the total of maintained and aided and those run by voluntary bodies, reached forty-four with over 2,000 children in attendance. Bradford experimented with a new type of joint nursery school and infant school for children aged two to seven. Leicester, London and Manchester were industrial cities that led the way in systematically improving conditions in nursery classes for three- to five-year-olds within infant schools, despite reduced grants for children under five. Leicester was able to include 27 per cent of three- to five-year-olds in nursery classes. In Manchester, where new infant schools were built with a nursery wing, there were sixty-six nursery classes by 1934 (Wood, 1934).

A typical nursery classroom at this period was furnished with light, movable tables and chairs, and folding beds for a midday rest. The room opened on a playground equipped with climbing frame, chute and see-saw and perhaps with a garden border. A class was twenty-five to thirty children within a year of the same age. Class activities included singing nursery rhymes, eurhythmic dancing, percussion and story-time. There was a regular routine to the day, with time allowed for free play. Toys and apparatus were carefully chosen for their educational value and children were encouraged to experiment with building, painting and other activities that promoted muscular control, sensory perception and healthy physical development. They were taught to wash, dress, use the lavatory and keep the classroom tidy.

But economic crisis intervened to prevent extension of this sort of provision. A White Paper in 1931 required cuts in public expenditure, and the Consultative Committee's recommendation in 1933 for expansion of nursery schools was ignored for three years.

Partial economic recovery indicated by a steady fall

in unemployment, at a time when there were empty infant classrooms because of a lower birth-rate in the Depression years, encouraged the Board of Education to issue a pamphlet in 1936 again urging the value of nursery schools or classes in areas where the home environment was unsatisfactory. When *Circular 1444* invited LEAS to survey their areas' needs for nursery education many responded with plans for limited expansion, mostly for opening nursery classes in infant schools: eighty-three LEAS produced schemes for 183 nursery classes, and further nursery schools were opened bringing the total of maintained and voluntary-aided to 114 by 1939.

TABLE 6   Children under five in maintained and aided schools

| | Infant & elementary | | Nursery schools | |
	aged 3 & 4	% of ages 3 & 4	Under 5	Schools
1930	159,335	13·1	1,431	30
1933	156,164	13·1	3,277	58
1935	165,854	14·2	3,747	65
1936	159,642	14·0	4,234	79
1938	165,203	15·9	5,666	103

Source: Board of Education, *Annual Reports and Statistics.*

The low birth-rate of the Depression years meant that even limited expansion of both types of nursery provision benefited a higher proportion of children under five. The number and percentage of children aged three and four in school rose slowly, and in the larger urban schools they were grouped in nursery classes where they were educated along the lines of the new nursery schools. In this context teachers evolved the idea of the nursery–infant school as the first stage of education for children aged three to seven.

Sporadic as expansion had been, and though accommodation was still about a third less than at the beginning of the century, by the late 1930s there seemed ground for

79

optimism. Moreover, the quality of nursery provision had greatly improved. Phoebe Cusden, at one time secretary of the NSA, wrote in her preface to *The English Nursery School* in 1938: 'There are indications that the progress of nursery education in this country will, during the next few years, proceed much more rapidly than has hitherto been the case.'

6

Progress in infant schools:
1900–39

The infant school gradually developed an ethos of its own in the course of the first third of the twentieth century. The continued presence of considerable numbers of under-fives in some urban schools no doubt encouraged this in the early period, and developments in child psychology gradually began to provide a rationale for infant education. As a generation of teachers who had not learnt their trade under the system of payment by results came into the infant schools, a more flexible approach became possible. Pressures for early formal instruction were further reduced when the statutory length of full-time education was increased at the upper end, first by the progressive elimination of part-time exemption and finally by extension to fourteen years. The English 'New Ideals in Education' movement brought together a variety of forces for reform, and was reinforced by the influence of the American 'progressive education' movement from the later 1920s. That compulsory education began at least a year earlier in Britain than in other countries forced English educationists to consider some of the implications of research findings in the development of young children. Thus the English infant school evolved as a unique institution.

Infant schools under the 1902 Act

Whatever their origin, infant schools and elementary schools with infant departments or classes were taken over by the 330 new local education authorities following the 1902 Education Act. With regard to finance and control they fell into one of two categories: board schools, almost all of which included many infants, were termed 'provided' schools and were wholly financed from public funds through the rates; the various voluntary societies' schools, most of which included infants and some of which were exclusively infant schools, became 'non-provided' schools whose running costs were similarly publicly financed but whose buildings remained the responsibility of their previous owners.

Infants under the age of seven years were by now invariably grouped in separate classes from the older children, except in very small one-teacher village schools; in some instances they already formed separate departments —in nine of the fifty-four schools in Leicester, for example. The proportion of infants in the school population was high, being over a third, and about half of them were under five. In the larger, urban schools it was therefore usual to divide the infants into two classes of those above and below the age of five, the younger class being still commonly known as 'the babies'.

Because of the lack of provision of nurseries or nursery schools, infant schools and departments continued to fill the gap, particularly in the poorest, urban areas; but because this was an unintended function, they seldom adapted in any significant way. Inspectors commented that infant teachers felt 'obliged to show "results" of their teaching' and began preparation for inspection in Standard I from the babies upwards, even though payment by results was no longer in operation. The 1893 *Circular 322* remained the only official guidance for teachers until the 1905 Code was issued: the former made a distinction between what should be expected of infants over and under five, but included word-building, number work with beads, shells and cubes as well as needlework for the youngest. Such specific guidance was easier to implement than the general principle of 'recognition of the child's spontaneous activity' and 'especial regard to the love of movement'. Large babies' and infants' classes of sixty to eighty reinforced formal teaching as the only practical solution to problems of class management. Direct Froebelian influence was slow to infiltrate state infant schools: London heads were unwilling to appoint teachers trained at the Froebel Institute for fear they would be unable to cope with large classes (Cd. 2726, 1905, 5).

A typical infant classroom in the early 1900s was still fitted with a fixed, tiered gallery in which fifty to sixty or more infants sat in rigid rows. According to one inspector, Miss Harrington, the curriculum still consisted largely of the three Rs taught by mechanical drill methods necessitating much rote learning. All were required to learn to write with the right hand, the left being firmly folded behind their backs. Letter cards were used for word-building, which was done through sequential numbered stages. Kindergarten exercises and 'occupations' usually had a place in the time-table, but the routine method of teaching the whole class to fold paper, stitch, assemble wooden cubes or lay out sticks in number patterns was quite contrary to Froebel's original intention and principles. 'Object lessons', with a visual aid from the store cupboard placed on the teacher's desk, could provide opportunity for informative discussion in the hands of a lively and imaginative teacher, but were often merely exercises in stereotyped questions and rote answers from the teacher's manual. On occasion the class was allowed to draw and crayon a picture of a duck, a flower or a sailing-boat—provided that all did this correctly so that the finished results were as nearly as possible identical. These were then displayed along the rear wall, behind the gallery. Drill and marching, sometimes to martial music, took place in the playground or central hall.

Galleries were beginning to be removed from the babies' rooms to allow more opportunity for controlled movement on the level floor space, as they were equipped instead with movable kindergarten desks. Sometimes these youngest pupils sat on benches in a horseshoe while the teacher read or told them a story. In the more progressive schools there were sessions of free play in the hall where a variety of toys were made available—wooden toys on wheels, hoops, skipping-ropes, dolls and dolls' houses, drums and even a rocking-horse. Where there were large numbers of two- and three-year-olds, some were penned in fixed seats with desks along the walls while others used the space in the middle for freer activities. Much time was invariably spent on formal class instruction in which the pupils were given an early grounding in the three Rs.

1905 Code and suggestions

Inspectors increasingly condemned much of this formal instruction, particularly for children under five years old. 'All teaching of the three Rs should be abolished, except incidentally' (Cd. 2726, 1905, 29).

The 1905 Code stated that the principle of a fixed standard of attainment in the three basic skills at seven years should either be discarded or 'at least be strictly subordinated to the more general aim of encouraging mental and physical growth and of developing good habits'. Short lessons of not more than fifteen minutes were prescribed for the older infants who should be 'trained to listen carefully, to speak clearly, to recite easy pieces, to reproduce simple stories and narratives, to do simple things with their hands, to begin to draw, to begin to read and write, to observe, to acquire an elementary knowledge of number' (Cd. 2579). Hand and eye training, which some kindergarten exercises and occupations promoted, was considered important for future skilled operatives of the industrial working class and was consequently still advocated by those who were pressing for manual training in the elementary school curriculum.

The publication in 1906 of a collection of John Dewey's essays, edited by Professor J. J. Findlay of Manchester University, brought the latest American pedagogy to the attention of British educationists. It was in America that the Froebelian kindergarten underwent the most thorough reappraisal 'in the light of the recent contributions of biology, sociology, and modern psychology to the science of education' (Wheelock, 1913). In *The School and Society* (1899) Dewey had interpreted Froebel on play and 'the instinctive, impulsive activities of children' with a simplicity that extracted the educational application from his symbolism and freed the kindergarten from dependence on the original exercises and occupations. The Committee of Nineteen's second Report in 1913 concluded that 'activity for its own sake' was acceptable for the youngest but that a more specific aim was necessary for older kindergartners, and defined the teacher's role as 'mediator, interpreter, or guide'. These Reports, *The Kindergarten: Theory and Practice*, were published in London when English Froebelians were themselves giving up the formalized 'gifts and occupations' in favour of 'activity methods' and a more integrated curriculum. The new Froebelian teachers, especially those trained by Miss E. R. Murray at Maria Grey College, were reinterpreting Froebel's principles in the light of John Dewey's work.

85

Experience in their free kindergartens also influenced their teaching in infant schools, and led them to postpone the three Rs beyond six years to the post-kindergarten or transitional stage. They reorganized their private, fee-charging schools into three distinct stages—kindergarten from three to six, transitional from six to eight, and school from eight years. This pattern was adopted by independent day schools with preparatory departments.

Even in 1902 R. E. Hughes optimistically claimed that 'in the best of the English infant schools a profound revolution of method has taken place during recent years' and that 'there is no part of the English educational system so brimful of real promise' (1902, 40). He also admitted that 'much of the old routine still remains'. A minor break-through seems to have occurred in infant education during the first decade of the twentieth century, and was reflected in the official handbook of *Suggestions for Teachers* issued in 1905. This stated (1905, 22):

> The leading principle which determines the methods of education suitable to early childhood is the recognition of the spontaneous activities of the children. These are immediately recognisable as a love of movement, a responsiveness to sense impressions, and a curiosity which shows itself in the eager questions of intelligent children ...
> The process of education up to five or six years of age consists in fostering their harmonious development, taking care, above all, that as little constraint as possible is put upon free movement whether of body or mind.

Though common practice was slow to change, new and freer attitudes were spreading and were fostered by the inspectorate and some of the training colleges. The more child-centred view of the infant school may have resulted from the belated realization of how inappropriate the old, formal instruction was for children under five years old who constituted over a third of the infant school population in 1900, and still accounted for nearly a quarter in 1910. Focusing attention on the more general social and psychological needs of these youngest pupils thereby opened the way to a reappraisal of infant education above the statutory age of five years. In 1911 Edmond Holmes, chief inspector for elementary schools, wrote: 'the atmosphere of the good infant schools is ... freer, more recreative, and truly educative than that of the upper schools of equivalent merit.' The developmental tradition was strongest in state infant schools, where it met least opposition from either the instructional elementary tradition or from the preparatory tradition which dominated the private sector: 'as regards facilities for the education of their "infants", the "classes" are unquestionably much less fortunate than the "masses"' (1911, 87).

The progressive movement

In the period immediately before World War I there was a growing dissatisfaction with many aspects of education in both public and private sectors, and a variety of groups were pressing for reforms of one kind and another. These came together in 1915 at the Conference of New Ideals in Education, held at the instigation of the Montessori Society. Committee members included prominent educationists with various allegiances: Homer Lane from the American 'progressive education' movement, which was inspired by Dewey; Edmond Holmes, who called himself a neo-Froebelian, was an active supporter of Montessori whose work he had seen in Rome four years before; Albert Mansbridge, representing the Workers' Educational Association, was a friend and supporter of Margaret McMillan; and Sir William Mather, who was chairman of the Froebel Institute. The conference characterized the new spirit in education as 'reverence for the pupil's individuality and a belief that individuality grows best in an atmosphere of freedom'.

The impact of Freud's work is apparent in that statement. Freudian psychology was just beginning to infiltrate the new education movement and became significantly influential in the post-war period. Pioneers of 'progressive education' saw the relevance of Freud's revelations about the significance for adult personality of early childhood experience, and could attribute the *malaise* of the civilized world to the hypocrisy and inhibitions of Victorian culture. Though the romantic image of childhood was shattered by Freud's deductions about the nature of children's drives for self-satisfaction, the naturalists were concerned to preserve children from unhappiness imposed by the adult world and recognized that a child should be allowed to develop as a child and not as a miniature adult.

Jung's explanation of anti-social behaviour as neurotic manifestations of thwarted creative impulses, and his theory of the unconscious, also directly influenced the progressive education movement. As it was obvious that infant teachers substituted for parents, Jungian psychology brought a better understanding of the importance of sound relationships between teachers and children in infant schools, and drew attention to other roles than the instructional. This accorded with the influence that nursery schools were bringing to the infant school.

Freud and Jung provided the final justification for condemning repressive and punitive methods, and persuaded infant teachers to accept childish sexual interests and agression. The developmental tradition in education was given a new connotation, particularly with reference to early upbringing and the infant school years.

Although not all the New Ideals group were politically conscious, the movement was linked with current left-wing social criticism and general disillusion with many aspects of contemporary society. Holmes, whose long experience in the inspectorate had made him a vehement critic of the contemporary education system, wrote in *What Is and What Might Be* (1911) of 'the spirit of Western Civilization, with its false standard of reality'. The Independent Labour Party, the Workers' Educational Association, several Trades Councils and the Trades Union Congress were actively concerned with educational reform at this time : in 1916 the 'Bradford Charter' was drawn up and adopted as policy by the Independent Labour Party and Labour Party conferences in 1917. Educational reform was widely promulgated in the educational and political press, and was concerned with school structure and the content of education at all levels from pre-school to university : much of it aimed at the regeneration of society through education.

In this it found close links with John Dewey's views on social education and the social function of education. Dewey argued the need to adapt schools to social conditions and to 'consider the relationship of the school to the life and development of the children in the school'. He attacked traditional schools 'for dealing with children *en masse*' instead of recognizing them as 'intensely distinctive beings'. His view of social education was close to Margaret McMillan's on the nursery school :

It is simply a question of doing systematically and in a large, intelligent, and competent way what for various reasons can be done in most households only in a comparatively meagre and haphazard manner. In the first place, the ideal home has to be enlarged. The child must be brought into contact with more grown people and with more children in order that there may be the freest and richest social life. Moreover, the occupations and relationships of the home environment are not specially selected for the growth of the child; the main object is something else, and what the child can get out of them is incidental. Hence the need of a school. In this

89

school the life of the child becomes the all-controlling aim (Dewey, 1899, 35-36).

This approach not only set a premium on social education, but required teachers to arrange for learning to take place through experience and 'by doing'.

The shock of the war, the impetus it gave to democratic aspirations and the desire to create a better world, brought many of these groups closer together in the New Educational Fellowship whose journal, *New Era*, was launched in 1920. In the private sector a number of experimental schools were founded, several of them taking children of all ages and all cutting across the age divisions that became established in the state sector. They did not, therefore, contribute specifically to the new concept of the infant school, though they exerted a significant indirect influence in favour of a more informal and permissive atmosphere. Infant teachers found much to interest them in the writings of A. S. Neill, in particular.

The climate of educational opinion after the war was receptive to ideas from the 'progressive education' movement in America. There theory and practice were being elaborated by Dewey and many others and, publicized by the Progressive Education Association from 1920, began to gain ground in the American public elementary school system. W. H. Kilpatrick was particularly influential through his development of 'learning by doing' into the 'project method'. Susan Isaacs, who contributed more than anyone else in Britain during this period to a scientifically based theory of infant education, wrote that Dewey 'always had a profound influence on my educational thought' (Gardner, 1969, 163). It was she who developed the logic of Dewey's theory for infant and nursery education, to which he himself paid relatively little attention since six was the usual starting age in American schools. Her position as head of the Child Development Department at the

London Institute of Education, and her numerous books and articles ensured that her influence on infant education was considerable. As one teacher said, 'She made a "bridge" for teachers between the work of educational theorists and classroom principles and practice' (Gardner, 1969, 169).

The child-centred infant school

The reduction in the proportion of under-fives in elementary schools to under an eighth of the total under seven by 1920 meant that infant teachers were able to focus attention on the specific needs of the fives to sevens. That the infant school, alone among schools in both the public and private sectors, was not under pressure from external and competitive examinations, left infant teachers freer to work out a new child-centred education in terms of the emotional, social and intellectual needs of their pupils. Susan Isaacs helped to provide the rationale, but for encouragement from accounts of classroom experience teachers drew on their American colleagues. The American experience of the common elementary school in a society at a comparable stage of industrial development offered teachers a realistic application of the new principles in working-class schools. *The Child-Centred School* (1928) by Harold Rugg and Ann Shumaker was a critical portrayal that English infant teachers found exciting in that it offered practical advice on the construction of a new curriculum for the 'activity school', using integrated 'centers of interest' and 'projects'. What could be done with American first graders aged six to seven was clearly applicable to top infants in England. Experimental schools, in the mid-1930s, such as the Raleigh Infant School under E. R. Boyce in Stepney, owed their inspiration to American experience as well as to Susan Isaacs at the Malting House School.

Progressive infant schools adapted a variety of experimental methods from America and Europe, many of them not originally intended for such young children. Carleton Washburnes' 'Winnetka Plan' and Helen Parkhurst's 'Dalton Plan', devised for American junior high schools in 1919 and 1920 respectively, were used with top infants: children carried out tasks or assignments set by their teachers to allow each child to proceed at his own pace and choose when to work on different areas of the curriculum. The Decroly Method from Belgium and Ferrière's 'biological curriculum' from France were studied with interest and were partly responsible for the introduction of nature study, pre-history, and craft-work: both were examples of the application of Jung's psychological theory that children recapitulate mankind's learning experiences in their imaginative play, and hence enjoy practising primitive crafts and re-enacting a primitive way of life. Infant teachers incorporated this idea into projects on cave man, for instance.

The child-centred infant school, with its corollary of more attention to individual needs and differences and teacher–child relationships, was difficult to implement with overlarge classes in classrooms intended for formal class instruction. New infant schools built in the later 1920s and 1930s were designed as modified versions of the open-air nursery school: one storey only, opening onto a playground with a flower border, they were light, colourful and airy, furnished with portable desks or tables and chairs. But classrooms were still self-contained and often too small for really free activity and lacked the space needed for ambitious project work, for the Board of Education decreed that infants required only nine square feet each instead of the ten square feet allowed older children (*Circular 1325, 1924*).

But combined with acceptance of the newly formulated notion of individual 'readiness' for the three Rs, the child-centred approach led some infant teachers to abdicate their function as teachers of reading. This was particularly likely in exclusively manual working-class districts where, brought up in homes without books and where parents might be barely literate, children showed no 'readiness' to learn to read if the initiative was left to them. The best infant teachers, who fully understood the rationale of this method of education, realized the necessity of structuring an environment to promote the desire to learn and of introducing some 'directed activities' and planned group work. Written labels around the classroom and 'look and do' cards, as recommended by Montessori, were intended to encourage a desire to read. Superficially at least, arithmetic was less of a problem as these children were used to dealing with money for shopping errands from a very early age.

Good infant schools of the 1930s were described by, for instance, E. R. Boyce (1939) and M. J. Wellock (1932). Though one of their principles was 'the *self-chosen activity* of the child', their teachers did not abdicate from the teaching function, but were alert to seize any opportunity for stimulating and widening the children's interests and learning experiences. They ensured that the curriculum included work in the basic skills through the activities they promoted, though without dictating these. Music, drama and nature study as well as speech-training games and language training featured within the new, free atmosphere. Work based on individual interests developed into class projects with top infants. Projects became a characteristic feature of work in top infant classes, and even with younger children, long before the method was taken up by junior schools. Some projects were very elaborate and aimed to integrate the whole curriculum : the centre of interest usually came from social or environmental studies and included much art and craft for model-making as well as practical arithmetic and imaginative writing. A wide range of children's own work adorned the walls, plants grew along the window-sills and small animals were kept as pets. Where a nursery class was attached to the infant school the learning process appeared as a continuum, and the new theory and practice of nursery education exerted a further liberalizing influence.

Opposition

The child-centred approach was much less successful in transforming infant education in the private sector, except in the new wave of progressive schools founded in the 1920s. The preparatory instructional tradition retained a strong hold and presented a more determined resistance in kindergartens and schools giving early primary education for the middle class because of pressures for results in the scholarship examinations for grammar school places and for common entrance examinations for admission to public schools: the former set a premium on performance in the three Rs and the latter meant that preparatory school boys had to be well grounded in these basic skills in order to begin Latin at about seven or eight years. This, and the fact that schools charging fees could afford the special apparatus, may account for their greater willingness to accept Montessori methods.

Backwash from the free place scholarship system also exerted a counter pressure in state schools, particularly in combined infant–junior schools. 'More attention was certainly paid to the instruction of children between the ages of 5 and 11' and 'once more the child's nose was forced back to the grindstone' (Richmond, 1943, 60).

While the inspectorate generally encouraged the child-centred school, there was opposition from some official quarters. Lord Eustace Percy, who was at the Board of Education after the war, wrote in his memoirs of the period 1924-9 (1958, 105):

Educational philosophy had become dangerously romantic since the war, the more dangerously so because it was
being encouraged by, for instance, the American school
of Dewey to clothe its romance in the trappings of
science and to dignify it by the title of psychology.
This romantic science felt most at home in the nursery
and infant schools. It aimed at civilizing children rather
than instructing them; and it assumed—*o sancta simpli-
citas*—that the social virtues need not be inculcated but
would develop naturally if only the child could be
brought to school young enough and protected to that
extent from the conditions of his home environment.
Its ideal was a nursery school place for every child
from the age of two.

This criticism epitomizes the conflict that had been
evident for over a century between the developmental
and instructional traditions in infant education. It shows
how vulnerable the former was to charges of utopian
romanticism when it relied unduly on empirical justification, as its results were so much less amenable to quantitative examination than was retention of factual instruction. Lack of a coherent rationale was a weakness of the
child-centred education of the inter-war period.

The Hadow Reports (1931 and 1933)

Official opinion had not been converted to child-centred
education when the 1924 Provisional Code was issued.
Within the next ten years, however, a marked change took
place which was clearly reflected in the Consultative Committee Reports of 1931 and 1933 under the chairmanship
of Sir W. H. Hadow. By then the upward influence of the
ethos of the nursery school was apparent in the statement
that 'any realistic view of education must consider the
infant school not as a place of instruction, but as an in-

structive environment in which the child, under the sympathetic care of his teacher, may cultivate his own garden' (1933, xviii).

In their report on *The Primary School* in 1931 the Committee considered arguments for and against division of primary education into an infant and junior stage and recommended separate infant schools for children under seven. Its terms of reference excluded 'children in infants' departments', but as soon as it completed that report it was asked to consider 'educational provision for children up to the age of 7 +'. Its report on *Infant and Nursery Schools* was published two years later.

The influence of experience gained in the limited expansion of nursery education and the recent emergence of child-centred infant schools was strong in many critical observations and recommendations on the infant stage for children of five to seven. Recognizing that the statutory age of five marked no significant developmental stage, infant teachers should follow the principles advocated for nursery schools; transition to junior school at 7+ was considered more significant. Having declared that the whole of primary education should 'be thought of in terms of activity and experience rather than knowledge to be acquired and facts to be stored', the Committee discussed this in terms of school subjects at the junior stage; but it considered the secular curriculum for infants under three broad headings—'natural activities' including play, 'expression training' including handwork, and 'formal instruction in the three Rs'. It concluded that the latter had no place in infant classes for children under six but that the curriculum for top infants should be equally divided between the three areas, apart from religious instruction which was governed by legislation. Rigid timetables were condemned in favour of allowing the individual teacher discretion to allocate time flexibly according to the children's interests, which should not be unnecessarily interrupted. Froebelian and Montessorian approaches were to be combined in the new infant school.

The developmental and instructional traditions were reconciled in a critical reappraisal of both:

> The spontaneous unfolding of certain inherited powers that accompanies growth in natural surroundings is not the only aspect of mental development, nor of itself will it carry the child far. Mental development also includes the acquisition of certain forms of knowledge and skill that are neither natural nor innate. In particular before an individual can take his place in the civilised world, he must acquire the use of certain instrumental subjects. Among these the 3Rs are the key to all the rest.

Reading was regarded as 'incomparably the most important' of these basic skills. Although formal instruction should not begin under six, children might begin learning as soon as they seem ready and interested.

There was consideration of the implications for the infant stage of recent research evidence on the physical and mental development of children under seven. Attention was drawn to the limited reasoning powers of even five- and six-year-olds, with a footnote reference to Jean Piaget; but Susan Isaacs was cited as suggesting that older infants' difficulties in understanding physical cause and effect resulted mainly from lack of earlier opportunity to experiment. As children of infant school age still learned through direct sensory perception they should be encouraged to observe, handle and make things. Binet tests were recommended for diagnostic, but not for classification, purposes: segregation of apparently retarded children in special classes was condemned in favour of individual remedial help. Indeed, any form of streaming in the infant school was deprecated, though the 1931 Report had advocated three streams in junior schools.

97

Class instruction was recognized as inappropriate for much of the infant programme, for which nursery methods should be adapted. A mixture of class teaching, individual work and teaching in small groups was therefore advocated. An important corollary was insistence on individual records being kept, as in nursery schools.

The 1933 Report reflected the great progress that had been made in infant education during the previous ten years or so. Its break from earlier and much contemporary practice was more marked than the 1931 Report on education over the age of seven. In effect, nursery–infant education was seen as a continuum even though combined nursery–infant schools were not generally recommended. At a time when the new child-centred approach derived principally from Dewey was at variance with the older mass instruction approach, and when Froebelian and Montessorian theories seemed also to conflict, the 1933 Report put forward a new synthesis in the developmental tradition with due attention to the instrumental significance of the basic skills at the infant stage.

Separate infant schools

The lengthening of statutory education to a total of nine years led many local education authorities to organize separate junior and senior schools with a break at eleven years even before the Consultative Committee recommended it in 1926. Separate infant schooling for children under seven had been practised since the 1820s and this age demarcation had been reinforced by the Elementary Codes and the system of Standards. Already nearly 70 per cent of five- to seven-year-olds were in separate infant schools : some had been founded as infant schools in the nineteenth century, some had been instituted as separate schools or departments by school boards, or pressure of numbers facing urban local education authorities in the early twentieth century had caused them to find this solution the most economic as it enabled them to make maximum use of existing buildings. In 1925 *Circular* 1350 recommended two separate and parallel mixed departments for children aged five to eleven as it considered a 'double break in the school life ... apt to produce excessive retardation'. However, three years later this opinion was rescinded in an official pamphlet entitled *New Prospect in Education*, in which it was stated that the balance of the argument now seemed to favour separate infant and junior schools. This view was endorsed more emphatically by the 1931 and 1933 Consultative Committees. The arrangement was recognized as impractical in most small village schools, but in towns about a further 5 per cent of infants were organized in separate infant schools by World War II.

That there were so many separate infant schools during the period when new approaches to infant education were being worked out undoubtedly facilitated the evolution of a specific infant school ethos unhampered by downward pressures from more formal junior schools. On the contrary, some were subject to the influence of their own nursery classes, and the pioneers of the new nursery education saw education up to the age of seven or eight as a continuum. Some urban infant schools grouped the children vertically in parallel classes instead of chronologically, and the one infant class of five to seven or eight years of age was common practice in small schools.

The new infant school was slow to supersede the old, and there were still many where children sat in serried rows of desks, though no longer in galleries. Compromise was common with the result that in some schools a sharp distinction was made between periods of formal instruction and those of 'free activity'. But the English infant school was acquiring a reputation in the western world in the decade before World War II.

7

War-time priorities:
1940-4

Mothers and pre-school children

Great strains were imposed on the family during the war
years by the fathers' absence, evacuation with consequent
sharing of homes and the break-up of the extended family,
mothers going out to work and general disruption of
normal family life even in areas not subject to air raids.
Families of all social classes in most parts of Britain were
affected and became more dependent on government social
services for support which in peace time would be given
by relatives or domestic servants. Mothers of young children faced different problems in evacuation and reception
areas, but suffered nervous strain whether from air raids
or from living in a billet. Financial hardship forced some
to go out to work as wage-earners to supplement service
allowances which were inadequate if the husband was in
the lower ranks. Though mothers of children under fourteen were never mobilized, there were official and social
pressures for them to engage in paid or voluntary civilian
war work: it is known that 12 per cent of mothers with
very young children were employed, and this figure does
not take account of the voluntary work that many middle-
class mothers undertook.

Government action was determined by two main considerations—to safeguard children's health and to release women for war work. Schools and the school medical service could be relied on to achieve both aims when the children were over five years old, but additional services were required for those under five. New welfare services were gradually established by official and voluntary agencies on an unprecedented scale for mothers and their pre-school children. Local authorities were offered 100 per cent grants from the Ministry of Health for setting up new nurseries in areas selected by the Ministry of Labour. The Board of Education was unable to accept responsibility for children under two, and it was thought administratively convenient to unify all pre-school and maternity welfare. From May 1941 the Ministry of Health undertook to co-ordinate the various medical, social and educational services provided for the under-fives by official and voluntary bodies.

The war-time nurseries scheme

The nursery centres scheme, which had provided a rudimentary form of nursery school in evacuee reception areas, was absorbed in the war-time nurseries scheme in 1941. There were three kinds of provision: full-time nurseries under a matron were open twelve to fifteen hours a day for children from a few months to five years old, with a trained nursery school teacher for those over two-and-a-half years; part-time nurseries under a teacher were open during normal school hours for children aged two to five years; the admission age to nursery classes in infant schools and departments was lowered to include two-year-olds. The peak of nursery provision was reached in the autumn of 1944 when there were 106,000 children in nearly 1,000 day nurseries and 102,940 in nursery classes in England and Wales, with a further 6,338 in Scotland's war-time nurseries. There were wide variations in standards of accommodation, facilities and activities dependent on availability of premises and staff and attitudes of local authorities. Wherever the choice existed, mothers showed a clear preference for nurseries and nursery classes over child-minders: in 1944 only 4,280 under-fives were being looked after under the Ministry of Labour's child-minder scheme.

The war-time nurseries scheme was a compromise that exposed divergent views on the aims of nursery provision. The scheme was regarded as a victory for the day nursery approach in which health was the prime consideration and pre-school education was only incidental. Protagonists of the nursery school feared it might prove a setback to the movement for nursery education. A clash of interests was often evident between matrons and nursery teachers in full-time nurseries.

Impact on infant schools

On the other hand, the presence of children under five years old in nursery classes of elementary schools in new areas convinced more infant teachers of the value of combined nursery–infant education and engendered a better understanding of the function of play in infant education. Nursery school methods had an impact on infant school practice in parts of Britain that had not experienced nursery schools before the war, but were priority districts for the war-time scheme as evacuee reception areas or centres for munition factories for which women workers were needed.

Experience in nurseries and schools, and official studies of the effects of evacuation, resulted in a sharp distinction being made between pre-school children below and above the age of two. There was general agreement that day-time separation from the mother below about two-and-a-half years was likely to be emotionally harmful, but above that age there were benefits in terms of social learning and development. The social pressures that induced middle-class mothers to undertake voluntary or paid war work, and the convenience of using the local state system when petrol rationing precluded daily transport by private car, meant that nurseries, nursery and infant classes catered for a much wider cross-section of social classes than in pre-war times. This experience gave support to the idea of the common nursery–infant school for all as the first stage in a democratic system of education.

Making a post-war policy

Policies were discussed and plans made for post-war reconstruction of the social services during the last years of the war. The case for large-scale nursery provision seemed sound and had wide support, but often in terms of a social rather than an educational service. During the war the focus had switched from the old urban slums to evacuation reception areas, and to the social rescue motive was added the war time expedient of releasing mothers for work. When a previous Parliamentary Secretary to the Board of Education said in the House of Commons, 'The war experience has proved to the country what Margaret McMillan proved to the few', he revealed his failure to appreciate her concept of nursery education: for the wartime nurseries scheme had not extended provision of nursery schools and classes beyond the 1938 level, though it had provided many more nurseries. Margaret McMillan's philosophy was as little understood as Robert Owen's had been.

The Nursery Schools Association issued a report which reflected the experience of many nursery and infant teachers (1943, 3):

No home can provide all the child needs after the period of dependent infancy, if he is to grow adequately in mind and character as well as in physique. For this period the nursery school should be the natural extension of the home and in its home-like informality provide an all-round education. . . . Many children who begin school at the age of five suffer considerable check in their physical and mental development—while they go through the painful process of learning, often too late, how to adjust themselves to the social life of a group of children.

As infant schools became more child-centred, and there was more widespread experience of nursery classes immediately before and during the war, the idea won favour that nursery–infant schools were the most suitable form of provision. 'Extending infant schools into nursery schools would unite the ideals of the nursery school with the best traditions of the infant school' (NSA, 1943, 6).

The 1944 Education Act

The nursery school lobby was influential in the discussions which preceded publication of the White Paper, *Educational Reconstruction*, in 1943. This declared 'that the self-contained nursery school, which forms the transition from home to school, is the most suitable type of provision for children under five. Such schools are needed in all districts, as even when children come from good homes they can derive much benefit, both educational and physical, from attendance at a nursery school' (Cd. 6458, 1943, 8). This was a victory for nursery education as against nursery care and the social rescue tradition, but experience of nursery–infant schools in serving the developmental needs of children up to seven or eight was ignored. The 1944 Education Act proclaimed the policy anticipated in the White Paper, but allowed for nursery classes in infant schools where this was more convenient.

Under Clause 35 of the 1944 Education Act a child was 'deemed to be of compulsory school age if he has attained the age of five years'; and under Clause 7 local education authorities were required to organize public education in three stages 'to be known as primary education, secondary education, and further education'. Infant education was thus subsumed in primary and was not defined. Clause 8(2)(b) also required LEAs to provide nursery schools or classes for children under five, but no guidance was given in the Act on how universal this provision was intended to be. Local 'development plans' had to be submitted by each LEA to the Minister showing how it proposed to implement the Act, and Clause 11(2)(e) specifically requested plans 'for meeting the needs of pupils who have not attained the age of five years'. At the time that LEAS were working out their plans, provision for under-fives was as follows: 1,535 war-time nurseries provided for 71,250 children, 370 maintained and 41 recognized voluntary nursery schools took a further 19,182 and probably another 180,000 (183,740 in 1947) were in infant classes.

The nursery infant school was not meant to be incorporated in the post-war education system, except where nursery classes were attached to primary schools as a local expedient. On the contrary, infant education was included in primary, which was the first stage of statutory education and began at the age of five. There was, however, a clear obligation to provide nursery education.

The public imagination was not fired by the idea of nursery education for all in the way it was by the idea of secondary education for all. In particular, the Labour movement was not won over to support the Nursery Schools Association's campaign, but directed its efforts to securing universal secondary education. Moreover, progressive educationists were more concerned to preserve the pre-war impetus for child-centred methods in infant schools than to argue the case for nursery education. Thus, while the desirability of universal nursery education was recognized, failure to incorporate it in the primary stage left it as vulnerable to economic squeeze as it had been after World War I.

8

Towards a rationale:
1945-70

Changing social patterns

World War II changed social patterns in ways that were significant for the upbringing of pre-school children of all social classes. Advances in technology and changes in the nature of industry and commerce in mid-century also contributed to new social patterns of equal relevance. Most important was the trend for more married women to work, and for them to do so in a much greater variety of occupations outside the home. Labour-saving domestic appliances, the design of modern homes and developments in the canned and frozen food industries combined to make it easier for them to make time for an outside job, and meant that many mothers found being a housewife was no longer a full-time occupation; and a generation of mothers who had benefited from secondary education, including a rising number who were further qualified, was likely to demand the satisfaction of at least a part-time job. During the war it was government policy to draw

married women into the labour force, and after the war
industry and commerce continued to need them. Inflation
and aspirations to raise family living standards further
encouraged reliance on two incomes among working- and
middle-class families. The effects of all these factors can
be seen in Table 7, which has been compiled from Census
material.

TABLE 7   Percentage of married women in employment

	1931	1951	1961
Occupied females over 14/15 years	16	40	52
Married women employed	13	23	30
Increase in number of women in professional occupations		+35*	+35†
Increase in number of women in part-time employment		+25*	+40†

(*since 1931; †since 1951)

By 1961 one in three of all married women had jobs,
either full-time or part-time. Studies in the early 1960s
found that between 12 per cent and 35 per cent of mothers
with children under five were working, and the Plowden
Committee's sample survey found 21 per cent. More recently, Viola Klein's sample survey found just over 7 per
cent of full-time and nearly 15 per cent of part-time married
women workers at forty-nine firms had children under five
years old (1965, 105). Though many married women tem-
porarily gave up work until their children were settled in
infant school, it was evident that many others resumed
work earlier. Investigations showed that more wanted to
do so, but were prevented because there was nowhere
to leave their youngest children. Post-war council estates
and the new suburban private estates fostered the trend
for young couples to set up home away from relatives,
where grandmothers were not available as child-minders.

The nuclear family gradually replaced the extended family across a much wider spread of social classes. The isolation of young mothers and their pre-school children in flats and on housing estates brought problems to which a nursery or nursery school might offer a solution.

Post-war housing shortages remained acute for several decades, especially in London, Glasgow, Birmingham and Liverpool. The 1965 White Paper on housing stated that 'some three million families still live either in slums, near slums or in grossly overcrowded conditions'. A substantial minority of young children were still brought up in circumstances of severe poverty and deprivation in a generally affluent society. *Circumstances of Families*, a government report published in 1967, revealed that well over a million children were in families below the poverty line as defined by the supplementary benefit scale. The need for nursery schools was urgent; but provision depended largely on voluntary effort and private enterprise except in areas covered by the Urban Aid Programme from 1969.

In these circumstances nursery provision fell far short of demand and need. A survey by the National Union of Teachers, *The State of Nursery Education* (1964), found two-year waiting lists for a third of existing nursery schools and classes, and estimated that 'the total demand for places ... exceeds supply in a ratio of eleven to four.' A sample study found that 70 per cent of working-class and 88 per cent of middle-class mothers would use nursery schools if these were available (Gavron, 1966, 69, 80). This unsatisfied demand extended far beyond the urgent needs of very poor families that the McMillans had campaigned about. Those needs were still not adequately met, as Simon Yudkin showed in his report published in 1967; and though the underprivileged of the slums were being steadily rehoused, many lived in high blocks of flats where their environment was constricted with little opportunity for young children to play.

As the nuclear family replaced the extended family, and as the number of children in a family stabilized at two or three, the young child's opportunities for social learning were reduced. High density urban living without adequate provision of safe play areas, and the great increase in the volume of motor traffic, brought dangers and imposed restrictions. Working mothers again had to deposit young children with local child-minders, often in conditions no better than in the previous century. Middle-class children were left with *au pair* girls who were no more qualified, and usually less experienced, than nineteenth-century nannies.

Deficiencies in pre-school experience were evident when children entered infant school. Socialization, encouragement of exploratory and imaginative play and the development of motor skills were tasks that the infant school, as it had emerged in the 1930s, was very willing to undertake.

The post-war primary school received far more middle-class children than the pre-war elementary school did, especially at the infant stage. This was a measure both of the effects of the Depression and post-war inflation on the ability of the middle class to buy private education, and of the improved reputation of education in state primary schools—again, especially at the infant stage. P. L. Masters found that 23 per cent of the boys who went to the Incorporated Association of Preparatory Schools' (IAPS) schools entered direct from local education authorities' primary schools, and that most entrants were between seven and nine years old (1966, 54-56). It is evident that state infant schools were used by a wider cross-section at the upper end of the social class spectrum than other stages of the state system, for only 16 per cent went to maintained secondary schools from IAPS schools. The infant school was the foundation stone for a comprehensive system.

From the middle 1950s the downtown twilight zones of the older cities were densely repopulated by Commonwealth immigrants, particularly from Cyprus, the West Indies, India and Pakistan. Multiple occupation of Victorian terrace houses was forced upon them by economic circumstances since most were in low-paid occupations. As English was often not spoken at home, lack of nursery schools meant that many entered school unable to speak much English and unfamiliar with various aspects of English culture. This imposed on infant schools tasks that would have been more appropriate to a nursery school. Infant schools in such districts were centres for learning to live in a multi-racial society.

Nursery education and the 1944 Act

The 1944 Education Act has been applauded for introducing secondary education for all and attacked for leaving the way open for this to be implemented by most local education authorities on a bipartite basis dependent on selection by an 11+ examination. Subsequent disappointments, when economies resulted in postponing or failing to implement certain clauses, also centred on secondary and further education. Yet primary schools, including infant schools, suffered from repercussions of 11+, and were more victimized than secondary schools by economies which damaged nursery education most of all.

There was much rejoicing at Clause 8(2)(b) of the 1944 Act which required local education authorities to plan with regard 'to the need for securing that provision is made for pupils who have not attained the age of five years by the provision of nursery schools or, where the authority consider the provision of such schools to be inexpedient, by the provision of nursery classes in other schools'.

Lillian de Lissa, for the Nursery Schools Association, noted that 'nursery schools have been given their proper place within the national system of education' (1945). And Violet Creech Jones, for the Fabian Society, was equally confident: 'So far as the nursery school is concerned, its future is now assured' for 'these schools ... are now recognised by the state as an integral stage in every scheme for universal education' (1945, 13).

These high hopes were betrayed by events. Not only did the intended expansion of nursery schools not occur, but in 1946 the Ministry of Health ceased paying 100 per cent grants for new day nurseries. There was a consequent resurgence of casual child-minding, often in conditions reminiscent of the old dame schools. Following press reports of scandalous circumstances, the Ministry of Health was given responsibility for the registration and supervision, through local authorities, of private nurseries and child-minders in the 1948 Nurseries and Child Minders Regulation Act. But there was much evasion of the law as reports and surveys revealed in the 1960s: these led to an amending Act in 1968, but enforcement remained erratic with much local variation. Illegal child-minding became prevalent in immigrant districts.

The way was opened for further exclusion of the youngest from infant schools when the 1948 Education (Miscellaneous Provisions) Act defined the statutory age for admission as 'the term after that in which they reach their fifth birthday'. Discretionary earlier admission was still permitted, but shortage of teachers and space caused many infant heads to apply the letter of the law. By linking infant and junior education together as primary, the first of the three stages of statutory education, the 1944 Act reversed the tendency to think of a nursery–infant stage as ideally the first stage, and to deny the Hadow Committee's recognition a decade before of a distinct infant stage. *Circular* 280, issued by the Ministry of Education in August 1954, stated that 'the Minister will expect the admission of children under five to be restricted or prohibited where their admission would stand in the way of a reduction in the size of over-large classes'. This was reiterated two years later, and again in 1960, when local education authorities were explicitly forbidden to allow numbers of under-fives attending school to rise. Coinciding with the halt on expansion of nursery schools, this reversed the trend of the late 1930s: in fact the proportion of two- to five-year-olds in maintained and grant-aided schools had fallen from 15·9 per cent in 1938 to 12·3 per cent in 1950, and to 10·2 per cent by 1965. That there was some flexibility in applying the restriction on four-year-olds once the post-war birth-rate bulge had passed through the primary schools can be deduced from the National Child Development Study of the 1958 cohort, which found that 'nearly half started school when they were aged four years six months to four years eleven months' (1966). Heads of infant schools, many of whom believed in the ideal of the nursery–infant school, were willing to admit younger children when they had enough room and staff: but they had neither in the 1950s when the post-war birth-rate bulge was passing through the primary schools.

As these children passed on to secondary education, the government determined that priority must be given to provision of secondary schools. *Circular* 8/60, issued in May 1960, made clear that an absolute prohibition must be maintained on expansion of facilities for nursery education: a two-shift system of part-time attendance at nursery classes was recommended as a means of accommodating more children under five without additional expenditure. With minor modifications this Circular defined policy for over a decade (see Table 8).

It is evident that considerable use was made of the shift system for part-time attendance, and that nursery schools increasingly took three- and four-year-olds rather than younger children. A declining birth-rate again enabled infant schools to admit more nursery children in the 1960s as in the late 1930s, but no extra money was allowed for

TABLE 8   Provision for children under five in LEA schools

	Infant schools & Departments	Nursery schools		
	Children aged 3 & 4*	Aged 3 & 4	Under 3	Schools
1946/7	183,740	19,048		370
1950	148,324	17,229	3,360	416
1961	180,754	18,754	2,253	453
1965	197,268	21,729†	1,920†	461
1969 Full-time	220,257	16,011	855	470
Part-time	22,626	14,402	668	

* figures include a high proportion who were nearly five.

† includes 7,925 part-time counted as 0·5 per child.

Source : DES *Statistics of Education.*

adapting classrooms. When the Central Advisory Council for Education, reporting on *Children and Their Primary Schools* (the Plowden Report) in 1967, recommended 'a large expansion of nursery education' on a mainly part-time basis for about two-thirds of all three- and four-year-olds, its advice was ignored except in designated Educational Priority Areas as *Circular* 8/60 remained in force. Only sixteen new nursery schools opened in the nine years after that circular.

The first sign of change was when the Urban Aid Programme was launched in January 1969 to provide over 10,000 extra nursery places in areas of greatest social need. Under the first two phases 10,626 new places in nursery schools and classes were approved that year, but no more in 1970 and only a further 5,000 in the third and final phase in 1971. These extra places were confined to designated EPAS: outside this programme expansion was still restricted under *Circular* 8/60 and its addenda. Even with nearly 16,000 UAP places the total in 1971 was less than

a third of the number that the Plowden Committee estimated would be needed by 1975.

The effect of the standstill since the war meant that the
1939 pattern in maintained provision was frozen, with
little opportunity for LEAs to respond to local socio-
economic change. The UAP may have slightly altered this
situation, notably in the West Midlands and the North-
West; but tradition exerts a strong influence, as instanced
in London and Leicester being among the three authorities
that submitted claims for the largest number of projects
under the first phase—and Leicester, with maintained nursery places for 19·9 per cent of two- to four-year-olds,
already had the highest provision in the country, as it did
before the war.

Private nursery education

Private nursery schools only very partially filled the gap
in maintained pre-school provision as the fees charged made
them largely the preserve of the middle class. Parents of
the professional middle class, among whom the quality
press and the paperback publishers found a receptive market for articles and books on child development, began to
seek nursery education for the year or two before their
child's fifth birthday entitled him to start infant school.
Widening opportunities for married women to resume or
take up professional careers, and economic pressures for
a second income, acted as further incentives. The private
sector responded during the 1960s by greatly increasing
part-time places, especially for three- and four-year-olds, in
day preparatory schools and departments and nursery
schools. In 1965 there were over 18,000 of that age attending full-time and about 1,000 part-time; by 1969 there were
17,000 full-time and nearly 15,000 part-time. Total private
nursery provision was in fact much higher, as these figures
do not include nursery schools for children under five

114

only, registered with the Department of Health: there were probably at least 2,000 small schools in this category. National and sample surveys in the mid-1960s found that a quarter to a third of children from the professional middle class attended nursery school.

The quality of private nursery provision varied greatly from traditional kindergarten and Montessori schools, through the educationally 'progressive' in the Malting House tradition to playgroups run on semi-amateur lines. Other middle-class alternatives were to employ an *au pair* girl as a cheap, untrained substitute for a Norland nanny or arrange for a child-minder.

The playgroup movement

The first pre-school playgroup was started in Marylebone in 1961. Through the efforts of Mrs Belle Tutaev, a national movement came into being within a year as the Pre-School Playgroups Association. The Nuffield Foundation gave it a grant of £1,500 in 1962, and the Department of Education and Science £3,000 a year for three years in 1966 so that a national adviser could be employed. By then 20,000 children, mostly aged three or four, were enrolled in about 600 playgroups, mainly in London and the Home Counties.

The movement spread fast so that by 1971 there were about 7,000 playgroups for 170,000 children, and the DES agreed to pay for a second adviser. Playgroups were not nursery schools, though more than half of them were run by a qualified supervisor. The PPA definition was: 'a group of six to thirty children aged two-and-a-half to five years who play together regularly daily or several sessions weekly', usually morning or afternoon only. Mothers helped on a rota and their participation was considered important. Though local initiative usually came from middle-class mothers, the playgroup movement spread to a few working-class districts too.

Playgroups in slums and twilight zones of big cities were pioneered by the Save the Children Fund which was running 120 groups in 1971, by adventure playgrounds, by the Greater London Council's free 'one o'clock clubs' for mothers and young children in parks and near tall blocks of flats during weekday afternoons, by local committees of the Council of Social Service and by other local community councils. None of these playgroups aimed to compete with nursery schools by offering nursery education in the full sense, but all provided stop-gap facilities for socialization and supervised play. They met a social need, and in doing so partly diverted attention from the educational need for which successive governments refused to accept responsibility.

Following the designation of Educational Priority Areas after the Plowden Committee reported in 1967, pre-school playgroups were opened experimentally for some of the most underprivileged children. The Social Science Research Council included some in its action-research projects in five EPAS, but no DES funds were available for continuing these after 1971 when the SSRC projects ended.

The inadequacy of voluntary action alone was shown in the report, *Priority Playgroup Project*, published in 1969 by the Advisory Centre for Education: in the Balsall Heath area of Birmingham only 200 of the 4,000 children of pre-school age attended playgroups. Kevin Shea's survey in Liverpool found a total of 240 full-time and part-time playgroup and nursery school places in 1970 for over 2,000 children aged three and four years in three working-class wards. Playgroups cannot be regarded as an adequate alternative to the universal provision of nursery education.

Day nurseries

Day nurseries as a permanent feature of maintained provision for pre-school 'children with special needs' because of home circumstances were established after the war, some as a survival of war-time nurseries, under the Ministry of Health through local health authorities. During the 1950s and 1960s they regularly catered for between 21,000 and 22,000 children, about two-thirds of whom were over two years old. They provided day care, not nursery education, and were open throughout the year and for longer hours than nursery schools. In 1965, 60 of the 143 local authorities in England and Wales ran no day nurseries, while only 10 provided more places in them than in nursery classes and schools (Blackstone, 1971, 91). Day nurseries remained outside the mainstream of maintained educational provision even after special schools were transferred from health to education authorities.

Infant schools and the 1944 Act

The decade following the 1944 Education Act brought significant changes to infant schools. Post-war rehousing programmes and slum clearance created new estates on the outskirts of towns where many local education authorities found it economic to build combined infant–junior schools, thus reversing the previous trend towards separate infant schools. There was seldom room in these new schools for children below the statutory age as they had to contend with the post-war birth-rate bulge. The proportion of separate infant schools declined from over 70 per cent in the pre-war period to 60 per cent by 1955 and 56 per cent by 1965 (Plowden, 1967, 99). The decline in provision of nursery classes, as the 'bulge' brought vast numbers of five-year-olds into overcrowded, urban and rural schools, also reinforced the tendency for the maintained sector to regard 5+ as the age at which education began.

This *de facto* trend ran counter to the theory, advanced by the Nursery Schools Association and steadily gaining ground, that education from three to seven or eight should

117

be regarded as a continuum. The Nursery Schools Association warned, 'One of the greatest dangers is lest the impetus towards creating the new type of infant school should be swept away in the development of the primary school for children of five to eleven' (1945, 4). The restriction on admission of infants before their fifth birthday meant a more precise age demarcation which was counter to both the theory and the earlier trend. That restriction also brought about an anomaly whereby length of infant education depended on the month of birth: a child's attendance at infant school ranged from six to nine terms.

The most damaging repercussion of the 1944 Act on infant education was the inadvertent introduction of streaming into infant schools and classes. The direct result of 11+ selection examinations for all was that the three-track system of ability grouping—recommended in junior but not in infant schools by the 1931 Hadow Report—became the much more rigid system of streaming. In accordance with the Hadow Committee's recommendations, infants had not usually been rigidly classified by ability on transfer to the junior school, allocation to one of three tracks being deferred till they were eight or nine years old. The 1933 Report, *Infant and Nursery Schools*, had advocated classes based on chronological age with parallel classes in large schools, and had specifically deprecated segregation by ability grouping. The 11+, however, brought increasing pressure for earlier classification in the junior school, and this in turn brought pressure on infant heads to classify their six-year-olds. Streaming thus spread down into the infant school, especially in combined infant–junior schools, as those who were teaching in the early 1950s remember: such terms as 'squirrels' and 'rabbits' were substituted for the more obvious 'A' and 'B' classification.

Streaming ran so counter to the established developmental and child-centred tradition in infant education that

118

infants were the first to benefit from the campaign for nonstreaming, which gained ground in primary schools from the late 1950s. The return to nonstreaming, and experiments with vertical or family grouping in classes comprising the whole infant age range, accelerated in infant schools as the developmental tradition was reinforced by a better understanding of Piaget's and Susan Isaacs' research, and by the work of sociologists. Even so, the Plowden Committee estimated 'that in a quarter to a fifth of infant classes, children of six are graded by attainment, in some schools grading begins even earlier' (1967, 284). Ability grouping within classrooms was a common practice in infant schools that claimed to be nonstreamed. The Committee came out in favour of nonstreaming in infant schools.

A nursery–infant stage

In addition to the social factors discussed earlier, the demand for nursery schools was fostered by new attitudes to the educational needs of three- to five-year-old children. These new attitudes derived partly from the work of the pioneer nursery and nursery–infant schools of the 1930s and research, but also from experience in the many wartime nurseries of various kinds. Dr Simon Yudkin said that through the 'tremendous development of nurseries, crèches, nursery schools and all sorts of things for children' during the war, 'the philosophy grew up that these little schools had all been a kind influence in helping mothers to look after the children'. By 1954 the idea was becoming accepted that not only did young children not need to be with their mothers twenty-four hours a day, but that both they and their mothers gained if the latter were released to pursue other interests some of the time (NSA, 1954).

Further research into early child development in the

decades after the war convinced more and more parents 'that three-to-five-year-olds need opportunities to extend their environment beyond their home ... opportunity to meet and mix with other children and adults, for space and play equipment and for care and education by skilled people' (Yudkin, 1967, 4). The nursery school was increasingly seen as complementary to any home and not just a substitute for an unsatisfactory one. This conclusion had been reached by many in the NSA before the war, and was reflected in their 1943 Report. When the war ended the NSA no longer campaigned for nursery schools in working-class areas only, but for nursery schools for all. In this they anticipated the post-war demand by the middle class.

In pre-war times deprivation was considered mainly in physical and material terms; but from about the 1940s child psychologists began to regard emotional deprivation as possibly more important, and recognized that this can occur in any social class. In the next two decades lack of linguistic and intellectual stimulus were also regarded as deprivation. Recognition of the importance of early cognitive development made possible a *rapprochement* between the developmental and instructional traditions in nursery–infant education, especially in the light of research into the cognitive learning process which was itself found to be developmental or sequential.

The desirability of a distinct nursery–infant stage for which provision should be made in one school was accepted by the NSA during the war. By the end of the war the NSA was advocating 'a new type of school for children under eight—a school that combines the best features of the nursery school with the new movement animating infants schools' (1945, 6).

This was the opinion also reached by the National Union of Teachers Consultative Committee (1949, 23): 'The Committee do not wish to differentiate between nursery and infant stages on educational grounds. It is regretted that

this difference exists administratively. It is their firm conviction that one type of education should cover the period
of early childhood, extending at least to 7 + .'

It advocated the spread of nursery methods, especially
'the approach to learning by way of active experience
and experiment', upwards into infant schools. In evidence
to the Plowden Committee, the NUT endorsed the views of
the NSA, in the belief that all counter arguments were
'outweighed, even in urban conditions, by the singleness
of purpose and uninterrupted study of the individual that
can direct the aim of a combined school' (1964, 10).

The limited number of infant schools and departments
with nursery classes was accumulating empirical evidence
to support the idea of combined nursery–infant schools.
Its advantages were fully exploited at the Eveline Lowe
School in Camberwell for children from three-and-a-half
to nine years old. There the youngest had their own nursery, but the rest were in 'family groups' within age ranges
of four to six and seven to nine. This school has been
described as 'an oasis of child-centred activity in a harsh
world of brick and mortar alien to their needs' (van der
Eyken, 1967, 94). It is organized largely on the basis of an
'integrated day', regards social integration and co-operation
as especially important and provides plenty of encouragement and help for writing, reading and number work.

Evidence from research

Educational research in the middle decades of the twentieth century provided rational justification for a child-
centred nursery–infant school. Psychological research
showed how intellectual development could be fostered
by an environment rich in opportunities for experiment
and exploration. Sociological investigation showed that
temporary absence from the mother was not harmful but
might even be beneficial in enlarging social experience,

and that children of working mothers were not worse off if appropriate nursery facilities were available. Further information on the harmful effects of the worse forms of child-minding, and how extensive it was, drew attention to the urgent need for nursery schools. Children who attended nursery school or started early at infant school were found to adjust and perform better at least in their early years at junior school: when streaming was common practice on entry to the latter this could have long-term importance for their future progress.

From Susan Isaacs' pioneer work, child development became the central field of study in infant teacher training and contributed to a better understanding of the pre-school and infant age group. Longitudinal and follow-up studies drew attention to the wide variations in all aspects of the development of children of the same age, and the uneven development of individual children. Educational psychology gradually became less exclusively concerned with mental measurement and widened the scope of its investigations, though it long remained dominated by American behavourism. Social psychology emerged as a discipline which stressed socialization as a function of nursery and infant education and, influenced by psycho-analysis, contributed to a sounder understanding of early emotional needs and growth.

Sociologists brought a new social science to bear on educational problems and, from the early 1960s, began to shed light on sub-cultural and class differences in child-rearing. The work of Basil Bernstein in England and Martin Deutsch in America drew attention to the significance of early linguistic development. In this they were influenced by the earlier work of A. R. Luria in the Soviet Union on the key role of speech and language in intellectual growth and the child's ability to form concepts.

Children of the manual working class were found to suffer disadvantages from their more limited linguistic experience as the language used by teachers in school followed characteristic middle-class patterns. It became obvious that nursery education could help to bridge the gap between home and school and between pre-school learning experiences of children from different social classes.

Of particular significance for nursery and infant teachers was the research of the Swiss psychologist, Jean Piaget. His early work had interested Susan Isaacs, though she was critical of his methods and felt he was too doctrinaire in some of his conclusions. His major contribution was the idea that young children pass through a series of sequential stages in their intellectual growth, each characterized by different types of mental response. Piaget's own work was descriptive, but his thesis was applied by others to the development of more structured teaching to suit the individual child's stage of learning. Pedagogical theory derived from Piagetian research supported learning by experience through discovery methods, but put a new emphasis on the importance of structuring this.

Studies in genetics and the bio-chemistry of the brain led to a better understanding of the physiological basis of learning in early childhood. At the same time, in the controversy over the relative influence of heredity and environment fresh doubts were cast on the prognostic validity of mental testing, without prejudice to the use of intelligence and reading tests for diagnostic purposes in infant schools. Improved techniques for early diagnosis meant that subsequent educational failure or backwardness could often be averted if defects in hearing, sight, speech, language development and minor cerebral dysfunction were ascertained during the pre-school years; but unless the child went to a state nursery school, class or day nursery, there was little likelihood of diagnosis until too late for effective remedial action.

Research in the mid-twentieth century began to explain

a great deal more about how children learn, both formally and informally, and generally supported methods that progressive teachers had been evolving empirically in the 1930s. What was new was an appreciation of the need to structure the learning process. By the late 1960s a new rationale was beginning to emerge. The Plowden Report in 1967 summarized much of the research of the previous thirty years and made it more readily comprehensible to parents and teachers.

The teaching revolution

'Experimental' or predominantly 'informal' infant schools were still in the minority in 1942 but had become common ten years later and, by 1966, 'very large numbers of infant schools give part of their time to periods of "free choice" or "creative activities"'. By then a pioneer minority had 'again gone ahead towards an even great flexibility in time-table' known as the integrated day (Gardner, 1966). But acceptance of the child-centred approach was not uniform. Another observer described the situation in 1955: 'Most of the galleries have now gone, but the gallery pattern of education dies hard, and in all too many of our infant schools one still sees young children seated, for most of the day, in static desks all facing the blackboard, receiving instruction rather than education' (Mellor, 1955, 28).

Dorothy Gardner's evaluations of 'informal' and 'formal' infant schools helped to establish confidence in the freer, child-centred schools. In several enquiries conducted over a period of twenty years, she found children from 'informal' infant schools were superior to those from the 'formal' control schools in tests for: listening and remembering, ingenuity, English (including writing an original composition or poem), free drawing and painting; and there was little difference in mechanical arithmetic. Guarded support was also given in the new official handbook *Primary*

Education, provided teachers were 'critically aware of what they are doing and of the value of what the children are learning' (Ministry of Education, 1959, 54).

Infant schools of the 1960s differed from the pioneer schools of the 1930s and common practice in the late 1940s in their rejection of the doctrine of 'reading readiness' in favour of 'more definite attempts to encourage all five-year-olds to start learning to read' (Gardner, 1966, 6). This change received support from a National Foundation for Educational Research (NFER) study which found that it was important to ensure children were secure in their ability to read by the time they reached the age of eight, as otherwise they were likely to remain retarded (Morris, 1966). The concept of 'reading readiness' or an appropriate mental age was exploded by Downing and Thackray whose research was published by the United Kingdom Reading Association in August 1971; they also found that tests were of far less value than the teacher's observations for deciding when to start teaching a five-year-old to read. Concern to make learning to read easier induced about 5 per cent of schools to use the initial teaching alphabet; there was much controversy over this in the 1960s. Infant teachers experimented with many methods, from phonics and various reading kits and programmed schemes to 'look and say', but generally settled for a mixed method which allowed flexibility in responding to individual children. Research tended to support teachers who tried to select methods for individual children rather than rely on any particular system.

It was not just the skill of reading that infant teachers were trying to teach earlier than had been fashionable in the 1930s and 1940s. It was part of a new appreciation of the importance of language. The new handbook, *Primary Education*, devoted a whole chapter to 'language' because it recognized that 'development of thought itself depends on a multiplication of names and a perception of the categories and concepts they imply' (Ministry of Education, 1959, 138). 'An informal introduction to reading and writing' was regarded as not inappropriate to the nursery school, once children 'have achieved reasonable confidence and fluency in speech'. Infant schools were expected 'to develop an environment in which the skills of reading and writing, though not disproportionately laboured, appear desirable to the children and a normal part of everyday life' (ibid, 149). The all-important role of language was even more fully appreciated by the time the Plowden Committee reported (1967, 210):

> Experience and language interact all the time; words come to life in the setting of sensory experience and vivid imaginative experience. It is equally true that experience becomes richer when talked over and recreated ... The achievement of many infant schools has been to build on and to extend children's experiences, to provide opportunities for talk about them and to create a warmth of relationships which encourages children to talk and to listen.

The *Breakthrough to Literacy* materials, introduced into infant schools from 1967, were based on these assumptions while allowing teachers maximum flexibility in how they used them. Like Montessori, the authors separated the skills of reading and handwriting: but, in direct opposition to her principle, they aimed to help children to compose and understand written language before acquiring the motor skill.

During the 1960s, when there was growing concern about the impoverished language development of children in the poorest home environments of big cities in Britain and the United States, pre-school language development was recognized as crucial. In accordance with the new principle of positive discrimination, systematic language instruction became an important feature of some nursery education programmes for downtown children. Pioneered by Carl Bereiter and Siegfried Engelman in America, the idea was tried out in Britain by the Social Science Research Council as a research project in five Educational Priority Areas, and the National Foundation for Educational Research adapted the American *Peabody Language Development Kit* through pilot trials in Slough nursery schools. No one knew whether early teaching of this kind would prove effective in the long term, but it aroused immediate hostility among English nursery and infant teachers committed to the Froebelian naturalist developmental tradition and a metaphysic of unfolding from within each child. Nursery education that admits of more structured teaching is in line with Montessori's approach to pre-school education in the slums. Conflict between the two approaches was resumed as vehemently as fifty years earlier, but with the important difference that official policy now inclined to favour more structured methods.

Several different types of structural apparatus for enabling children to acquire number concepts began to be used in infant schools from the 1950s, though most were designed for juniors rather than infants. A mathematical rather than an arithmetical approach characterized this teaching revolution. Piaget's descriptions of chronological stages in ability to form concepts dominated teaching in this area during the 1950s and 1960s: easily fitting the 'readiness' approach, they tended to discourage not only rote learning but also attempts to accelerate understanding, and infants were often left to sort out their confusing experiences somewhat haphazardly. By the early 1970s there were indications of critical reconsideration of this approach and its results. Some of the influences responsible for this change were Jerome S. Bruner's work, American experiences of direct teaching in pre-school programmes for underprivileged children and Peter Bryant's team at Oxford. Infant teachers began to recognize that language and number work were more closely related than had been supposed, and were more generally critical of the whole 'readiness' doctrine.

Renewed attention to the three Rs in the child-centred infant school and a few nursery schools was not a return to the ethos of the elementary tradition. Both the developmental and the instructional traditions had matured: both had taken an understanding of the learning process into account, the one as a facet of intellectual growth and the other as a means to more effective teaching techniques based on sequential learning. That post-war infant schools were catering for more middle-class children, whose parents welcomed the informality and free activity that allowed them to develop as unique individuals and at the same time expected them to learn instrumental skills in preparation for subsequent stages of education, may have been partly responsible for this meeting of previously parallel and sometimes hostile traditions in infant education.

Need for reappraisal

The conflict was not explicitly resolved because the rationale of English child-centred education, with its characteristically busy classroom, remained implicit having evolved pragmatically without much attention to theory. It was on the basis of this pragmatism that structural apparatus, kits and programmes were accepted into infant schools alongside free activity. When teachers did not appreciate underlying theories contradictions occurred: ability grouping round tables in supposedly nonstreamed classes, subject-centred displays and rotation of subject-oriented activities under the name of integration, individualized learning that not only prevented socialization and co-operation but also widened achievement differentials, group seating as rigid as the old rows in galleries, congenital defects unnoticed because masked by intelligent behaviour and quiet introverts neglected in the extroverts' classroom. Much was achieved, but the time had come for an appraisal of current practice and belief.

From 1969 a backlash attack was launched on 'progressive' methods in a series of *Black Papers*, some of whose criticisms were a serious challenge to trends in infant education from the early 1930s answerable only if the implicit rationale was made explicit, inherent contradictions and conflicts resolved.

That conflict of aims was sharpest with regard to nursery education is understandable in historical terms. Nursery schools were first advocated in 1905 as a means of removing young children from the pressures of elementary schooling, and were later developed as a rescue operation in the slums. Circulars in 1922 and 1960 ensured that they retained the latter function, and the playgroup movement reinforced the notion that opportunity for socialization and play was all that was needed. The content of nursery education consequently changed little over fifty years, and attention focused on the practical problems of extending provision rather than on developing theory.

Most of the scant provision for children under five years old had occurred in nursery classes attached to infant schools. In 1969 there were nearly 200,000 more three- and four-year-olds in nursery classes than in nursery schools in the maintained sector, and over 30,000 more in such classes in the private sector. Five was never the age of demarcation in the latter, where the kindergarten from three to six or seven was long established. If nursery classes became an accepted rather than an *ad hoc* part of infant schools and departments the way would be open for working out a rational theory of nursery–infant education; but official policy militated against this by severely restricting LEAs from providing the opportunity. A professional approach was threatened by the growth of voluntary playgroups, which by 1970 catered for more than three times as many under-fives as were in part-time attendance at nursery schools and classes throughout the maintained and independent sectors together: they cover an estimated 5 per cent of the age group. Nevertheless, the slowly growing number of infant schools with nursery classes were in the best position to undertake the necessary empirical research into nursery–infant education as a continuum: in the NFER, Schools Council and SSRC appropriate bodies now existed to further this, and the new philosophy of education developed by Richard Peters and Paul Hirst were attempting to clarify aims implicit in child-centred education.

The Plowden scheme

A hundred years after the passing of the Forster Education Act for universal provision of elementary schools the case for universal availability of nursery education was irrefutable. The Plowden Committee recognized the need and recommended immediate expansion with the ultimate aim of universal provision and voluntary attendance 'from the beginning of the school year after the age of three' (1967, 126).

Nursery schools from the days of the McMillans had been envisaged as taking children aged two to five, and strong arguments had been advanced in favour of combined nursery–infant schools for those aged two to seven: but from the 1950s there was a tendency to delay admission to three years (Ministry of Education, 1959, 28). The social-developmental tradition of nursery education gradually transformed the first year of infant education from the 1930s so that an infant reception class closely resembled a nursery class; but the influence of new approaches to teaching number and language caused post-war infant schools to promote more structured and specific learning from about six. Experience increasingly led infant teachers to question the Hadow demarcation between infant and junior at seven, and to suggest that continuity in learning and teaching methods was needed up to eight. A consensus among nursery teachers, playgroup supervisors and parents now distinguished between the social need for care in nurseries for a minority of children under three and the desirability of nursery education for all over three of four.

This rethinking was reflected in the confused interim and long-term recommendations of the Plowden Committee. The two-tier Plowden scheme was for 'nursery groups' from three to five and 'first schools' from five to eight, entry at each stage being from the September after the relevant birthday. The upward extension to eight was welcomed by infant teachers, but many doubted the advisability of the two-tier scheme and a deferred start at infant school. Some feared that nursery groups might be more like playgroups than nursery schools, with consequent dilution of nursery education. The Committee did not argue the case for or against nursery–infant schools, but recognized that initially nursery groups would 'often be in existing primary schools'.

The Plowden scheme ignored experience gained of nursery classes in infant schools during the thirties and sixties. Never officially recommended as the ideal form of provision, nursery classes nevertheless educated thousands more than nursery schools. They offered certain advantages in enabling infant teachers to meet and know about the children, thereby facilitating continuity, and in avoiding the sometimes unsettling experience of starting school at five in totally unfamiliar surroundings. The transformation of infant education through the middle decades of the century nullified the case made by the women inspectors and the Consultative Committee in the early 1900s for removing under-fives from school. Nursery–infant education had become viable.

Socio-political factors

Socio-economic pressures and popular demand were forc-
ing the issue of nursery provision to the political fore-
front by the early 1970s. A variety of organizations joined
together in 1965 to form the National Campaign for Nursery Education. Once again all political parties promised
expansion in their election manifestoes. The middle-class
Women's Lib movement took up the demand; SSRC projects, the UAP and designation of EPAs highlighted the issue
in working-class districts. Lack of nursery provision and
the activities of playgroups were recognized by the press
as newsworthy, and the quality papers ran feature articles.
Where, journal of the Advisory Centre for Education,
devoted increasing attention to pre-school education and in
June 1971 put forward a policy for a phased attack on
the problem. Anxious to divert public attention from the
issue of comprehensive secondary schools, the new Conservative Secretary of State attempted to focus interest on
the hitherto neglected primary schools and promised a review into education for the under-fives. It became clear
that if Circular 8/60 were withdrawn, most LEAs would be
under considerable local pressure to implement Clause
8(2)(b) of the 1944 Act and the spirit of the Plowden Report.

An analysis of maintained and independent nursery education available in the various administrative regions of
England and Wales in 1965 was published in 1971. It
showed a tendency for more maintained provision in industrial and more independent in middle-class residential
areas, and for relatively high and low provision by either
sector to be complementary; but there were regions where
both were very sparse and nowhere was combined provision adequate to meet demand (Blackstone, 1971).
Regional variations were as marked as those of school
retention beyond fifteen years : that variation determined

the government to raise the statutory leaving age to sixteen rather than rely on voluntary staying-on. A child's opportunity for pre-school education depended on where he lived and his parents' social class.

For while maintained provision continued to be tightly restricted, the private sector expanded and PPA playgroups multiplied. Maintained provision was quantitatively slightly greater and qualitatively more uniform than private; but in a situation where only about 20 per cent of children had access to any nursery facilities, the role of the private sector was significantly greater at pre-school level than in the school system as a whole.

TABLE 9   Provision for children under five in 1969

Maintained:	
in infant schools and departments	243,151
in nursery schools	31,946
in day nurseries	22,030*
Total	297,127
Private:	
in preparatory departments	11,468
in nursery schools (listed by DES)	1,788
in nursery schools, nurseries and playgroups	
registered as 'premises'	196,100*
Total	209,356
with child-minders as registered 'persons'	69,055*
Children aged 2 to 5 years	2,524,000

*includes some under 2 years

Source: DES *Statistics of Education* for 1969, Department of Health and Social Security *Annual Report* for 1969.

Charges in the private sector ranged from 10p to 30p per half day and ten guineas or more per term, several surveys showed that a higher proportion of middle-class than working-class children attended nursery schools, and playgroups were predominantly middle-class. The effect was *de facto* discrimination in favour of middle-class children whose home environment was anyway likely to be more favourable to early learning experiences. Restriction in the public sector combined with market forces causing *laissez-faire* growth in the private sector was widening the gap between the social classes in terms of pre-school learning, and hence imposed greater burdens on infant schools which had to try to equalize educational opportunity.

The child-centred infant school faced a dilemma: committed to nonstreaming it received children who had already been streamed in their pre-school years; committed to fostering individual growth in the developmental tradition with due attention to natural learning sequences it found some children had to be taught what others had already learned at nursery school or at home.

Differences in home environment and early upbringing were enhanced by patterns in the availability of nursery education. The infant school had become the cornerstone for a comprehensive education system, but its effectiveness and that of the school system as a whole was undermined without universal nursery education. The case was generally conceded but commanded a low political priority. Meanwhile, infant schools with nursery classes exploited their opportunity to work out a rationale of nursery–infant education in practice. Nomenclature and philosophy have changed but the nursery–infant school has been in the making for a century and a half as a unique British institution.

Further reading

Historical accounts of educational developments

The most comprehensive, straightforward account of nursery and infant education is in the first chapter of the Hadow Report, *Infant and Nursery Schools* (HMSO, 1933), which has now been reprinted by Cedric Chivers Ltd. General histories of education do not differentiate education and provision for younger children from elementary, but there is a fair amount on infants in J. W. Adamson's *English Education 1789-1902* (Cambridge, 1964 ed.), and G. A. N. Lowndes puts education in a social setting and pays more attention than others to nursery education in *The Silent Social Revolution* (Oxford, 1969 ed.). Provision for under-fives since 1850 is surveyed by T. Blackstone in *A Fair Start* (Allen Lane, 1971) which considers trends from 1945 to 1965 in some detail. The nineteenth-century infant school movements are discussed in some detail by H. Silver in *The Concept of Popular Education* (MacGibbon & Kee, 1965), and there are descriptions of infant schools of the same period in *The Education of the People* (Routledge &

Kegan Paul, 1967) by M. Sturt. There is some historical material from the early 1900s in the National Union of Teachers' Report, *Nursery–Infant Schools* (1949). In *The Pre-School Years* (Penguin, 1967), W. van der Eyken has chapters on the early pioneers, on social needs and neglect since the 1920s and on the post-war changing environment. The various conflicting traditions are discussed with some references to infant education by W. A. C. Blyth in *English Primary Education*, vol. 2, *Background* (Routledge & Kegan Paul, 1967). The best source of information on nurseries and nursery schools during the second world war is *Studies in the Social Services* by S. Ferguson and H. Fitzgerald (HMSO and Longmans, 1954).

Social background

Relevant social background of the early industrial revolution is contained in *England in Transition* (Pelican, 1953) by D. George, and the Victorian era by G. Kitson Clark in *An Expanding Society: Britain 1830-1900* (Cambridge, 1967). For the twentieth century there are sections on socio-economic matters in *England in the Twentieth Century* (Pelican, 1965) by D. Thomson, and in a more journalistic vein in *The Age of Illusion, 1919-40* (Penguin, 1964) by R. Blythe. A useful introduction to economic development is *An Economic History of England, 1870-1939* (Methuen, 1960) by W. Ashworth. Students whose general historical background knowledge is limited will find a text book for the whole period useful, such as *Modern Britain* (Longmans, 1950) by D. Richards and J. W. Hunt.

Educational theory

Most so-called histories of infant education concentrate on the ideas of the great educators : a useful one for the nineteenth century is *Infant Schools, Their History and*

Theory (1904) by D. Salmon and W. Hindshaw. This can be supplemented with the later chapters of *The Origins and Growth of Modern Education* (Pelican, 1970) by E. Lawrence. For a fuller understanding it is necessary to read selected writings by these pioneers and to consult studies of individuals. The following are recommended : chapters 1, 2, 7 and 25 of *Practical Education* by M. and R. L. Edgeworth (1789 or later editions); *Pestalozzi: his Thought and its Relevance Today* (Methuen, 1967) by M. R. Heafford; *Robert Owen on Education* (Cambridge, 1969) edited by H. Silver; *Friedrich Froebel, A Selection from his Writings* (Cambridge, 1967) by I. M. Lilley and *Friedrich Froebel and English Education* (Routledge & Kegan Paul, 1969) by E. Lawrence; John Dewey's *The School and Society* has been reprinted by Phoenix Books as a paperback, and is the most relevant of his writings for infant education and his reinterpretation of Froebel; chapters 12 to 15 in any edition of M. Montessori's *The Montessori Method* (Robert Bentley in the United States, 1964) and *Maria Montessori, Her Life and Work* (Hollis and Carter, 1957) by E. M. Standing; *Margaret McMillan, 'The Children's Champion'* (Museum Press, 1960) by G. A. N. Lowndes; *Susan Isaacs* (Methuen, 1969) by D. E. M. Gardner. An account of the Malting House School is given in *Adventures in Education* (Allen Lane, 1969) by W. van der Eyken and B. Turner, and her *Teachers' World* articles are published as *The Children we Teach* (University of London Press Unibooks, 1970).

Articles

The ninteenth-century infant school movements have been discussed by W. P. McCann in 'Samuel Wilderspin and the Early Infant Schools', *British Journal of Educational Studies*, vol. xiv, no. 2 (1966) and by D. A. Turner in '1870 : The State and the Infant School System', BJES, vol. xviii, no. 2 (1970). R. Szreter's article, 'The Origins of Full-time

Compulsory Education at Five', BJES, vol. xiii, no. 1 (1964) is also useful.

Filmstrips

There is illuminating visual material on social background and life in schools, including nursery and infants, in *The Silent Social Revolution* compiled by G. A. N. Lowndes. He has also made *The Life and Times of Margaret and Rachel McMillan*. Both can be obtained from him at 29 The Green, Marlborough. Much of the material in this book is illustrated in *Nursery and Infant Education* by N. Whitbread (Visual Information Services Ltd, 12 Bridge Street, Hunderford, Berks.).

Bibliography

ADAMSON, J. W. (1930), *English Education 1789 to 1902*, Cambridge University Press; reprint 1964.

BAILEY, M. E. (1876), *Hints on Introducing the Kindergarten System into English Infant Schools*, George Philip.

BARTLEY, G. C. T. (1871), *The Schools for the People*, Bell & Daldy.

BIRCHENOUGH, C. (1925), *History of Elementary Education in England and Wales from 1800 to the Present Day*, University Tutorial Press.

BLACKSTONE, T. (1971), *A Fair Start: the Provision of Pre-School Education*, Allen Lane.

BOARD OF EDUCATION (1904), *Report of the Inter-Departmental Committee on Physical Deterioration* (Cd. 2175).

—— (1905), *Reports on Children under Five Years of Age in Public Elementary Schools, by Women Inspectors* (Cd. 2726).

—— (1905), *Code of Regulations for Public Elementary Schools* (Cd. 2579).

—— (1905), *Suggestions for Teachers*, HMSO.

—— (1908), *Report of the Consultative Committee upon*

the School Attendance of Children Below the Age of Five (Cd. 4259).

—— (1913), Statistics of Public Education in England and Wales, Part I (Cd. 7674).

—— (1921), Circular 1190.

—— (1924), Circular 1325: Size of Classes.

—— (1926), Circular 1350: Organisation of Elementary Schools.

—— (1926), Circular 1371.

—— (1927), Handbook of Suggestions, HMSO.

—— (1928), New Prospect in Education, HMSO.

—— (1931), Report of the Consultative Committee on The Primary School, HMSO.

—— (1933), Report of the Consultative Committee on Infant and Nursery Schools, HMSO.

—— (1912-13, 1930-8), Annual Reports and Statistics.

—— (1940), Circular 1495: Nursery Centres.

—— (1941), Circular 1553: War-Time Nurseries.

—— (1942), Circular 1609: War-Time Nursery Classes.

—— (1943), Educational Reconstruction (Cd. 6458).

BOYCE, E. R. (1938), Play in the Infants' School, Methuen.

—— (1939), Infant School Activities, Nisbet.

BURGESS, H. G. (1958), Enterprise in Education, SPCK.

CHARITY ORGANISATION REPORTER (1872), Nos 22, 28, 29, 30.

COLE, G. D. H. & POSTGATE, R. (1938), The Common People, Methuen.

COMMITTEE OF COUNCIL ON EDUCATION (1840-1, 1846, 1854-5), Minutes.

COVENEY, P. (1967), The Image of Childhood, Penguin Books.

CUSDEN, P. E. (1938), The English Nursery School, Kegan Paul, Trench & Trübner.

DAVIES, N. R. (1940), Ten Years' History of the Chelsea Open-Air Nursery School, 1929-1939.

DE LISSA, L. (1945), Education Up to Seven Plus, Nursery Schools Association, Publication No. 59.

DEPARTMENT OF EDUCATION AND SCIENCE (1961, 1965, 1969) *Statistics of Education.*

—— (1960), *Circular 8/60; Addendum* No. 1 (1964); *Addendum* No. 2 (1965).

DEPARTMENT OF HEALTH AND SOCIAL SECURITY (1969), *Annual Report.*

DEWEY, J. (1943 ed.), *The School and Society*, University of Chicago Press.

DOBBS, A. E. (1919), *Education and Social Movements*, Longmans.

DOWNING, J. & THACKRAY, D. V. (1971), *Reading Readiness*, Allen & Unwin.

EDGEWORTH, M. & R. L. (1822 ed.), *Essays on Practical Education.*

EDUCATION ACT (1944), (7 & 8 Geo. 6, Ch. 31).

EDUCATION DEPARTMENT (1893), *Circular 222: Instructions for Infants.*

—— (1897), *Special Reports on Education Subjects*, Vol. 1.

ELLIS, A. (1968), *A History of Children's Reading and Literature*, Pergamon.

FERGUSON, S. & FITZGERALD, H. (1954), *Studies in the Social Services*, HMSO & Longmans.

FRY, A. (1838), 'The Junior School of Bruce Castle, Tottenham', *Central Society of Education Papers*, 243-249.

GARDNER, D. E. M. (1942), *Testing Results in the Infant School*, Methuen.

—— (1949), *Education under Eight*, Methuen.

—— (1950), *Long-Term Results of Infant School Methods*, Methuen.

—— (1966), *Experiment and Tradition in Primary Schools*, Methuen.

—— (1969), *Susan Isaacs*, Methuen.

GAVRON, H. (1966), *The Captive Wife*, Routledge & Kegan Paul.

GEORGE, D. (1953 ed.), *England in Transition*, Pelican.

GIBBS, M. A. (1960), *The Years of the Nannies*, Hutchinson.

GREAVES, J. P. (ed.) (1827), *Letters on Early Education*, Gilpin 1850 ed.

HEAFFORD, M. R. (1967), *Pestalozzi: His Thought and Relevance Today*, Methuen.

HECHINGER, F. M. (ed.) (1966), *Pre-School Education Today*, Doubleday, New York.

HERFORD, W. H. (1905), *The Student's Froebel*, Pitman.

HEWITT, M. (1958), *Wives and Mothers in Victorian Industry*, Rockliff.

HILL, F. (1836), *National Education: its Present State and Prospects*, Charles Knight.

HOLMES, E. G. A. (1911), *What Is and What Might Be*, Constable.

HUGHES, R. E. (1902), *The Making of Citizens*, W. Scott.

INTERNATIONAL KINDERGARTEN UNION (1913), *The Kindergarten: Theory and Practice*, USA.

ISAACS, S. (1930), *Intellectual Growth in Young Children*, Routledge & Kegan Paul.

—— (1970 ed.), *The Children We Teach*, University of London Unibooks.

—— (1933), *Social Development in Young Children*, Routledge & Kegan Paul.

JACKSON, B. & RAE, R. (1969), *Priority Playgroup Project*, Advisory Centre for Education.

JONES, I. (1929), 'Infant Education—Prospects and Pitfalls'. Paper delivered at the North of England Conference.

JONES, V. C. (1945), *Nurseries and Nursery Schools*, Fabian Research Series No. 89.

KITSON CLARK, G. (1962), *The Making of Victorian England*, Methuen.

KLEIN, V. (1965), *Britain's Married Women Workers*, Routledge & Kegan Paul.

LAWRENCE, E. E. (1912), *Types of Schools for Young Children*, Froebel Society.

LAWRENCE, E. (ed.) (1969), *Friedrich Froebel and English Education*, Routledge & Kegan Paul.

LILLEY, I. M. (1967), *Friedrich Froebel, A Selection from His Writings*, Cambridge University Press.

LOG BOOKS OF KING RICHARD'S ROAD SCHOOL, LEICESTER (1880-1900).

LOVETT, W. & COLLINS, J. (1841 ed.), *A New Organisation of the People, Embracing a Plan for the Education and Improvement of the People, Politically and Socially*, 1969 reprint, Leicester University Press.

LOWNDES, G. N. A. (1969 ed.), *Silent Social Revolution*, Oxford University Press.

—— (1960), *Margaret McMillan, 'The Children's Champion'*, Museum Press.

MARSH, D. C. (1965 ed.), *The Changing Social Structure of England and Wales, 1871-1961*, Routledge & Kegan Paul.

MASTERS, P. L. (1966), *Preparatory Schools Today*, A. & C. Black.

MARVIN, F. S. (ed.) (1908), *Reports on Elementary Schools 1852-1882, by Matthew Arnold*, HMSO.

MCCANN, W. P. (1966), 'Samuel Wilderspin and the Early Infant Schools', *British Journal of Educational Studies*, vol. xiv, no. 2.

MCMILLAN, M. (1923 ed.), *Education Through the Imagination*, Sonnenschein.

MELLOR, E. (1955), *Education through Experience in the Infant School Years*, Blackwell.

MICHAELIS, E. & MOORE, H. K. (trans, 1866), *Autobiography of Friedrich Froebel*, Allen & Unwin.

MILLER, E. W. (1944), *Room to Grow!*, Harrap.

MINISTRY OF EDUCATION (1947), *Circular 155: The Educational Building Programme*.

——, *Annual Reports and Statistics*.

—— (1951), *Education, 1900-1950* (Cd. 8244).

—— (1954), *Circular 280: Reduction in Overlarge Classes*.

—— (1956), *Circular 313*.

—— (1959), *Primary Education*, HMSO.

—— (1960), *Circular 8/60: Nursery Education* and Addendum No. 1 (1961); Addendum No. 2 (1965).

MINISTRY OF HEALTH, *Annual Reports*.

MONTESSORI, M. (1964), *The Montessori Method*, Robert
Bentley, Mass., USA.

MORRIS, J. M. (1966), *Standards and Progress in Reading*,
NFER.

MORTON, A. L. (1962), *The Life and Ideas of Robert Owen*,
Lawrence & Wishart.

NATIONAL EDUCATION UNION (n.d.), *A Verbatim Report of the
Debate in Parliament during the progress of the Elementary Education Bill, 1870*.

NATIONAL UNION OF TEACHERS (1949), *Nursery Infant
Schools*.

—— (1964), *The State of Nursery Education*.

—— (1964), *First Things First*.

NURSERY SCHOOLS ASSOCIATION (1943), *The First Stage in
Education*.

—— (1954), *The Needs of Young Children in Present Day
Society*.

OWEN, R. (1813), *A New View of Society*.

—— (1836), *The New Moral World*.

PARKER, E. (1898), 'Preparatory School Assistant Masters',
Longman's Magazine, 31, 330-46.

PARLIAMENTARY PAPERS (1820-34), P.P. 1820, xii; 1831-32,
xv; 1833, xx; and 1834, ix.

PATTERSON, A. T. (1954), *Radical Leicester*, University College, Leicester.

PERCY, SIR EUSTACE (1958), *Some Memories*, Eyre & Spottis-
woode.

PLOWDEN COMMITTEE (1967), *Children and their Primary
Schools*, HMSO.

POLLARD, H. M. (1956), *Pioneers of Popular Education*, John
Murray.

PORTER, S. (1838), 'On Infant Schools for the Upper and

Middle Classes', *Central Society of Education Papers*, 229-42.

POVERTY (1967), Journal of the Child Poverty Action Group, no. 4.

RICHMOND, W. K. (1943), *Blueprint for a Common School*, Routledge.

ROBSON, E. R. (1877), *School Architecture*, Murray.

RUGG, H. & SHUMAKER, A. (1928), *The Child-Centred School*, New York, World Book Co.

RUSK, R. R. (1933), *A History of Infant Education*, University of London Press.

RUSSELL, B. (1946 ed.), *On Education Especially in Early Childhood*, Allen & Unwin.

SALMON, D. & HINDSHAW, W. (1904), *Infant Schools, their History and Theory*, Longmans.

SELLECK, R. J. W. (1968), *The New Education, 1870-1914*, Pitman.

SIIEA, K. (1970), *Liverpool and its Under Fives*, Association of Multi-racial Playgroups.

SILBER, K. (1960), *Pestalozzi, the Man and his Work*, Routledge & Kegan Paul.

SILVER, H. (1965), *The Concept of Popular Education*, MacGibbon & Kee.

—— ed. (1969), *Robert Owen on Education*, Cambridge University Press (for extracts from his autobiography, 1857).

SKEATS, H. S. (1861), *Popular Education in England: being an abstract of the Report of the Royal Commissioners on Education with an Introduction and Summary Tables*, Bradley & Evans.

STANDING, E. M. (1957), *Maria Montessori, her Life and Work*, Hollis & Carter.

SZRETER, R. (1964), 'The Origins of Full-time Compulsory Education at Five', *British Journal of Educational Studies*, Vol. xiii, no. 1 .

VAN DER EYKEN, W. (1967), *The Pre-School Years*, Penguin.

VAN DER EYKEN, W. & TURNER, B. (1969), *Adventures in Education*, Allen Lane.

WELLOCK, M. J. (1932), *A Modern Infants' School*, University of London Press.

WHEELER, O. A. & EARL, I. G. (1939), *Nursery School Education*, University of London Press.

WHEELOCK, L. (1913), Preface to *The Kindergarten: Theory and Practice*, International Kindergarten Union.

WILLIAMS, R. (ed.) (1968), *May Day Manifesto 1968*, Penguin.

WOOD, G. M. (1934), 'The History and Development of Nursery Education in Manchester and Salford', unpublished M.Ed. thesis, University of Manchester.

YUDKIN, S. (1967), *0–5: A Report on the Care of Pre-School Children*, National Society of Children's Nurseries.